D0520834

CHOOSING A
COLOR SCHEME

CREATIVE HOMEOWNER PRESS®

CONTENTS

COPYRIGHT © 1992 CREATIVE HOMEOWNER PRESS®
A DIVISION OF FEDERAL MARKETING CORP.
UPPER SADDLE RIVER, NJ
This book may not be reproduced, either in part or in its entirety, in any form, by any means, without written permission from the publisher, with the exception of brief excerpts for purposes of radio, television, or published review. Although all possible measures have been taken to ensure the accuracy of the material presented, neither CREATIVE HOMEOWNER PRESS nor Eaglemoss Publications Limited is liable in case of misinterpretation of directions, misapplication or typographical error. All rights, including the right of translation, are reserved.

Based on Creating a Home,
First Edition © Eaglemoss Publications Limited 1986, 1987, 1988

Printed at Webcrafters, Inc.
Madison, Wisconsin, U.S.A.

Current printing (last digit)
10 9 8 7 6 5 4 3

Creative Director: Warren Ramezzana
Editor: Kimberly Kerrigone
Copy Editor: Carolyn Anderson-Feighner
Cover Photograph: Phillip H. Ennis Photography
Cover Interior Designer: Samuel Botero Associates
Design Consultant: Eve Ardia, ASID, Saddle River Interiors

Library of Congress Catalog Number: 91-071688
ISBN 0-932944-98-1 (paper)

CREATIVE HOMEOWNER PRESS® BOOK SERIES
A DIVISION OF FEDERAL MARKETING CORP.
24 PARK WAY
UPPER SADDLE RIVER, NJ 07458-2311

INTRODUCTION

With this book as your guide, you can plan colorful and imaginative decorating schemes for your home with all the confidence and flair of a professional interior designer. Forget about safe decorating schemes and dull furnishings. Armed with a basic knowledge of how color, light, pattern and texture work together, you can create exciting and adventurous schemes without the fear of making expensive mistakes.

Choosing A Color Scheme is packed with color photographs showing dozens of different room schemes, with captions explaining what makes them work. Color drawings demonstrate how different approaches can make the same room look radically different. And numerous color photographs of wallcovering, fabric and floorcovering swatches show in detail what has been used in the main picture, or demonstrate the effect of putting particular colors and patterns together.

The first chapters cover the basic principles of working with color, and explain such mysteries as using a color wheel and how to create a sample board. Plus, the ultimate professional touch: designing each room so that it is visually continuous with the next.

How to create three distinct schemes based on harmonious colors, contrasting colors and neutral tones enlivened with accent colors follows. Additional chapters explain the practical aspects of color, such as how to make rooms seem large or small, light or dark, warm or cool. A series of photographs demonstrates how the same colors change when seen in daylight and artificial lighting.

How to pick patterns is presented in the same practical way, with pages of full color illustrations. These show how to analyze different types of pattern, how to coordinate patterns with colors, how to use mini prints and how to mix and match patterns. The final section covers textures, which is the third design element.

Choosing A Color Scheme is an invaluable ideas book to use every time you plan a new decorating scheme.

THREE WAYS TO A COLOR SCHEME

Does choosing a color scheme pose problems? Here are three ways to help you get it right.

Color is probably the most useful of all the tools at the decorator's disposal. Handled properly, it can make a small room seem larger, a dark room lighter, or bring about a complete change of atmosphere.

Whether you're creating a color scheme from scratch or updating an existing one, it's important to plan it properly. Take your time, get ideas from other people's color schemes – in homes, offices or even restaurants – and make a note of those colors that you find satisfying and pleasing.

Before you commit yourself to a particular color, sit down and work out what kind of look you are aiming to achieve. Start by defining the mood you want to convey – it might be warm and cozy, cool and airy, bright and cheerful, restful, pretty or stylish. Then think of which colors convey that mood. For example, warm pinks and reds create a cozy atmosphere, while cool pastels and whites give an airy, spacious feel.

Choosing colors and putting them together is partly a matter of taste, although there are general guidelines that can prove helpful.

First of all, *colors look different in different types of light.* A red that has a distinctly blue tinge in a showroom under strip lights may lose its blueness and appear a warm clear red when seen in a sunny room. A rich blue used in a dark room will appear even richer, but that same blue used in a brightly lit room can lose much of its intensity. So it is important to try out a large sample of the color in the room in which it will be used.

Second, *a color affects the colors next to it.* You may adore a certain pink and a certain green, but together they might prove disastrous. On the other hand, you may find a gray or beige dull on its own, but perfect when partnered with a lively splash of bright pink or orange.

This leads directly to the third point: *how much there is of a color affects how you see it.* An entire room of bright pink or orange may be hard to live with, but small concentrations of those colors can make an all-white room 'sing.'

If you find choosing colors and patterns a little confusing – and most of us do – on the following five pages you will find three approaches to color scheming, each using a different starting point.

Matchmaking

There may be furniture, carpets or curtains already in the room you want to decorate, so use them as a starting point. The decorative scheme shown on the next page is based on this carpet sample.

The 'theme' scheme

The room above has a predominantly blue scheme but there are other colors used, all derived from samples assembled around the blue theme.

Most of the wallcoverings and fabrics here are dappled or textured for added interest and to counteract the cold quality that flat blue paint sometimes has.

Note how lighting affects the colors – the spotlights in this room make the colors less bright than the samples seen in daylight conditions (opposite).

POINTS OF DEPARTURE

Few of us have the luxury of being able to create a room scheme from scratch. You may be stuck with a major investment that can't be changed easily – a carpet or sofa, say – around which you have to plan. This can be turned into an advantage, though, because it gives you a starting point from which to work. Overcoming limitations can be a great incentive.

Collecting samples One way to avoid expensive mistakes is to try out your chosen colors and patterns by collecting samples – like those opposite – so that you can see how they work together.

Start by finding a sample of the fixture you can't change (if you can't find an exact match for your own carpet, for example, look for one that's close to it in color and texture).

Now start collecting scraps of fabrics, wallcovering, colored wools and so on, in the colors you want to combine with your 'permanent fixture.' (You will find that it helps if one or two of the samples incorporate a bit of the 'fixture' color to help tie it all together.) The current trend for coordinated lines of fabrics, wallcoverings and borders makes this all much easier. You will also be able to determine whether the amount of

pattern is appealing or too busy.

Mix and match Don't restrict yourself only to one range of tones. A room with light apricot walls, mid-apricot furniture and a dark apricot carpet may match perfectly, but is also in danger of looking dull and flat. With imagination, any color can be interpreted in many different ways. Blue, for example, can be 'true blue,' blue-green or blue-violet – it can also be light or dark, pale or intense.

Subtle patterns mix and match more easily than strong, large-scale ones. Here mini-pattern and Berber-weave carpets meet the practical need for a carpet pattern without being too dominant.

The texture of a sample is also important. The blue of a cotton weave may be exactly the same as that of a shiny ceramic vase, but both 'read' differently.

Collecting samples will help you get the feel of how to vary your theme color in interesting ways. Get a good collection of samples together, then start whittling down the choice to your final selection. Finally, you can experiment with small bits of contrasting or intense accent color to see which adds the right 'zest' that brings the whole scheme to life.

Variations on a theme
When collecting samples, remember to look for different surface textures and aim to incorporate one or two accent colors, too. Here the blues and blue-greens work well with either the gray or beige carpet – but notice how touches of terra-cotta and the mellow maple of the picture frame bring it all to life.

9

TAKE AN EXISTING PATTERN

Professional fabric designers are expert at handling color, so if there is a strong pattern on the carpet, walls, curtains or upholstery, follow the designer's example and use those colors as the basis for your scheme.

The color scheme of this room (left) is based on the upholstery fabric of the sofa (right). The pale apricot background color becomes the background color for the walls and curtains. The cool gray-blue in the pattern is echoed in the carpet and tablecloth, while the warm terra-cotta is used as an accent color, in the lamp shade, book bindings, table underskirt and cushion covers.

The off-white fabric pattern is repeated in the coffee table, shelves and paneling, to provide a welcome touch of freshness and stop the scheme from looking too heavy.

A pattern can tell you which colors go well together, but it can also suggest in which proportions they work best.

Look again at the picture on the left and you can see how this works in practice. The largest color area in the pattern – apricot – is also the largest in the room. The second most dominant area, the carpet, picks up the gray-blue. Likewise, the accents of white and terra-cotta are used sparingly to avoid overpowering the main colors. Proportion is an exercise in subtlety and color patterns will give you the key to a successful scheme.

By choosing such a harmonious blend of colors and tones, the owner has created a room that is elegant, restful and easy on the eye.

◁ *The 'pattern' scheme*
Taking the sofa covering as a starting point, this room's color scheme is derived purely from the fabric pattern – apricot, gray-blue, terra-cotta and white.

Notice, too, that the colors are used in similar proportions; the apricot is the main color and the gray-blue the secondary one, while others act as accents (right).

BRIGHT IDEA

COLOR CUES

Use patterned fabric as a guide when deciding where and how much of each color to use in a room.

Work out roughly how much of each color is used in the pattern – the largest areas of color, right down to small accent colors. Now list the parts of the room to be 'colored,' from the largest areas, walls and floor, to small accessories.

But don't stick too rigidly to the proportion idea. The dominant colors will depend on the room's size and available light; a dark color on the walls may not be advisable in a small room, for instance.

 In the fabric, mid-green is the main color; **carpet** is the largest area.

 The 'key' fabric used for the **curtains**, ties the scheme together.

Pale green is the next main color; **walls** are another main surface area.

 Pale wooden **furniture** echoes the pale browns in the fabric.

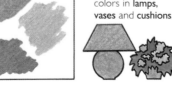 Brightest colors in the fabric are used as accent colors in **lamps, vases** and **cushions.**

 A pale, muted blue is used on the **bedspread.**

Finding inspiration

Cut out and collect pictures of rooms that you find appealing; this way, you can pinpoint which colors you feel comfortable with and use them as a basis for creating your own color schemes.

The gold and apricot tones of the magazine photographs (left) were the inspiration for the bedroom scheme (above). Soft yellow walls, an apricot carpet and creamy lace curtains create a warm, mellow mood, enhanced by subtle accents of clear pink and off-white.

FIND YOUR PREFERRED COLORS

You may subconsciously have a favorite color or color scheme but be unable to put it into words. Or perhaps you are confused by the vast choice of decorating colors.

To overcome this problem, collect as many interior decorating books and magazines as possible. It doesn't matter if some are out of date, or don't feature many examples of the type of room you're planning to decorate, so long as they contain plenty of color pictures.

Quickly thumb through them all, ignoring the style of the particular rooms, but marking the color schemes of those that appeal to you. When you've finished, put it all away and out of your mind.

Return to the books and magazines you selected a week later. You may be surprised to find that most of the pictures you selected have one or more colors in common and that frequently those colors are used in a similar way. By pinpointing your preferences, you can use this information to plan your ideal color scheme.

Remember that colors you may like to wear are not necessarily colors you can live with!

THE LANGUAGE OF COLOR

Understanding color will give you the confidence to create successful color schemes.

Different color schemes can make the same room seem cozy or elegant, soothing or stimulating, dramatic, even playful – and can even appear to alter the room's proportion. But perhaps because there are so many choices, it is often hard to know where to start.

The way professional designers talk about color can make it sound very complicated. But once you understand the basic principles of color theory, you'll be able to create color schemes with confidence and achieve exactly the mood and effect you want.

THE COLOR WHEEL
It is said that the human eye can distinguish over 10 million different colors. But every single one is based on the colors of the rainbow – red, yellow, orange, green, blue, indigo and violet – plus black and white.

To show how these basic colors relate to one another and how they combine to make all the other colors, scientists have come up with the color wheel.

Primary colors The three key colors are pure red, pure yellow and pure blue. They are known as primaries, because you cannot mix them from other colors. All other pure colors can be mixed from primaries.

Secondary colors Orange, green and violet are mixed from equal amounts of two primaries. In between come any number of intermediate colors – dozens of different yellow-greens, blue-greens, blue-violets and so on – all mixed from their neighbor colors.

Contrast colors Colors that contrast most strongly are directly opposite one another other on the wheel – red and green, yellow-orange and blue-violet, for example.

Harmonious colors These lie next to one another on the wheel. They share a common base color – for example yellow-orange, orange and red-orange all have the color orange in common.

Pastels, shades and mixtures The color wheel is shown in pure colors (i.e. colors that are created from a mixture of only two neighboring colors). Of course fabrics and paints and carpets also come paler (less intense) or lighter (with a mixture of white, known commonly as pastel). They come 'muted' or 'shaded' – with a mixture of gray or black. Or they come in subtle mixtures where a hint of color from another part of the wheel is added – yellow-orange with a touch of blue, or a hint of red added to yellow-green.

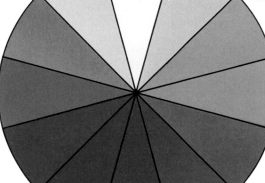

▷ *The color wheel*
The wheel is a useful tool for understanding how colors relate to one another and how to combine them in color schemes.

▽ *Secondary colors*
Pure green is made from equal amounts of yellow and blue; violet from red and blue; and orange from red and yellow.

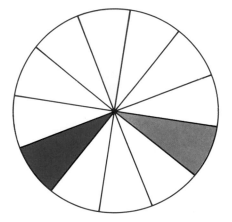

△ *Primary colors*
The color wheel shows how primary colors – pure red, yellow and blue – divide the wheel in three equal parts.

Warm colors

Reds, pinks, oranges, yellows – the colors associated with sunshine and firelight – create a cozy, welcoming atmosphere. Choose these warm colors – on the left-hand side of the color wheel – to make a large room look smaller and friendlier, to brighten up a sunless room, or simply because you want a warm effect.

Warm peach walls, pink patterned curtains, rusty red tones in the carpet and a mass of cushions in pinks, reds and yellows set the scene in this cheerful living room. The touches of white and cool green foliage of the plants help to balance the warm colors and prevent them from becoming overpowering.

When planning a warm scheme remember that the closer the color is to a 'warm' primary (red or yellow), the stronger it is. Large amounts of such colors can be hard to live with, so it's often wiser to choose their softer cousins, such as pink, peach and primrose yellow, reserving the stronger colors for accents only.

Cool colors

The other half of the color wheel is made up of greens, blue-greens and blues – the colors of cool water and shady forests, azure skies and dappled meadows. These are the colors to use if you want a room to have a cool, calm atmosphere.

The living room shown here has a distinctly tropical flavor: the various shades of cool blue used on the walls and seat coverings evoke the sea and the sky, and are perfectly complemented by the pale, sandy colors of the furniture and flooring, while the plants add accents of lush green.

Cool colors always appear farther away than warm ones. That's why cool colors make a small room appear more spacious, by 'pushing back' the walls. Be careful, however, if the room faces away from the light – cool colors here could look too bleak. Rooms that benefit from a lot of natural light can take almost any of the cool colors without appearing cold.

Contrasting colors

You can brighten up a room by using a contrasting scheme that features colors opposite each other on the wheel – for example, red and green, or blue and orange. These pairs of colors are known as 'complementaries.' When placed close together, they intensify each other, and the result is lively and vibrant.

In this room scheme the colors have been chosen to create a cheerful, sunny effect. Contrasting colors – red and green, blue and yellow – appear in the wallcovering, paint job and furnishings. The use of white is refreshing and accentuates the bright colors.

Contrasting colors used in equal amounts tend to produce an uneasy effect because they compete with one another, so make sure that one color dominates. Here, the yellow sofa provides a focal point that pulls the whole room together. The green area of window is smaller, while red is only used in small touches.

Harmonious colors

If you pick two, three or four colors that lie next to one another on the color wheel, you can be sure that they will combine comfortably because they are closely related.

Examples of harmonious groups of colors include pink, apricot, peach and gold – or clear blues, blue-green, aqua and green – or bluebell blue, mauve and heathery purple. They work together because nothing clashes or dominates and there is a common theme between one color and the next.

The room scheme on the left dispels the myth that 'blue and green should never be seen.' Fresh minty greens, blue-greens and emerald greens are layered upon one another, with the colors of the room echoed in accessories such as the lamp and vases.

The reds and yellows in the sofa fabric provide a touch of warmth to offset the cool effect created by the greens and blues; a small accent of contrasting color like this is a clever way to add pep to a harmonious scheme.

Pastel colors

Pure colors lightened with a lot of white are known as pastels. For example, red lightened with white becomes pink, pure green becomes apple green, orange becomes apricot.

These soft, gentle colors – sometimes called 'ice-cream' or 'sugared almond' hues – are always popular, since they look so fresh and pretty. They blend effortlessly with the lighter range of muted colors and with modern and traditional styles of furnishing. It is also interesting to note that any pastel color will coordinate with another – even opposites on the color wheel. This is because all the colors have a common element in that they contain a lot of white.

The light, airy and romantic style of this living room is achieved through the generous use of fabrics in pale blues and greens.

Subtle and muted colors

Pure colors that are darkened with black or gray are known as 'shades' or 'muted colors.' Then there are the more subtle colors that are a mixture of two or more pure colors – for example, orange with a bit of blue. But there is nothing dull about colors with such evocative names as russet brown, mustard yellow, sage green, petrol blue, or 'crushed berry' reds such as plum, mulberry and blackberry. Think, too, of the rich, exuberant lacquer colors inspired by the East – crimson, emerald green and gold.

Here muted colors create a cozy, autumnal feel. A variety of subtle and muted colors is used – browns and terra-cottas offset by cool greens and blues.

Because muted colors contain an element of black, they look particularly striking when teamed with black accents. However, you also need to introduce a sprinkling of brighter colors to prevent the scheme from becoming too heavy.

Neutrals

In the home designer's terms, neutrals range from white, through to creams, beiges, tans and browns, and from the palest silver gray through to black. They are useful for combining with more definite colors and you can also use them to create all-neutral schemes.

Inspiration for neutral schemes can be found in the earth colors of nature. Think of the bleached white of sand, the soft browns and tans of earth and wood, and the yellowed white of ripening corn.

The group of neutral-colored textiles shown here echoes the colors and textures of natural objects such as shells and pebbles, marble and wood. Textures and surfaces play an important part in any neutral scheme, since they add variety and interest.

Neutral colors are easy to live with, and provide a perfect foil for interesting furniture, pictures or plants.

Tones

When you're decorating a room, it's important to think about the range of tones. Tone describes the lightness or darkness of a color, as illustrated by these pink, red and maroon samples in light, medium, and dark tones.

A room containing only light and dark tones can look disjointed and broken – so remember to include some mid-tones to link the lights and darks and give the scheme more flow. (In the group of samples, see how deeper pinks and muted reds link the very pale pinks and maroons).

To understand how tone works, think of a black-and-white photograph, where colors are converted into black, white and gray tones. Now imagine a room decorated entirely in light-toned colors. Boring and bland, it would photograph virtually as the same shade of gray. By using a range of tones – whatever the colors – a room scheme becomes more satisfying.

ACCENT COLORS

It's amazing how small touches of bright and contrasting color bring a room to life. Most color schemes – particularly ones based on neutrals – benefit from the addition of an accent color. Accents need to be handled carefully though; two or three patches, not a dozen. Otherwise the effect becomes spotty.

Contrast accents

A room that is predominantly one color (monochromatic) needs a few accents to add pep and interest. The color wheel provides a handy, at-a-glance guide to choosing appropriate contrast colors – simply pick one (in this case, blue) from the side opposite the dominant color (yellow).

Sharp or bright accents

When the scheme is based on a pattern printed in several colors, it's usually effective to pick one color, then go for the touches of a brighter or more intense version of that color. In this scheme, bright pink piping on the curtains and table mats gives style and zest.

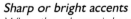

18

WHOLE HOUSE COLOR SCHEMES

When faced with four or five rooms to decorate and furnish at once, visual continuity is the secret of success.

▽ *Color inspiration*
This grand entrance with its cream colored walls and marbled floors sets the tone for the rest of the house. Oriental rugs and dark wood bannisters contrast with the light and airy feeling of this entryway. The flower arrangement, oil painting and trompe l'oeil lilacs add color while tying the scheme together.

Professional interior designers consider visual unity very important. Experience enables them to see the whole of a house interior as one interrelated, complete decorating unit rather than a series of separate rooms. Viewing in this way helps avoid a lack of continuity.

In small homes where space and light are usually a concern, creating a light, neutral-colored background using different shades of white, cream, beige and gray in walls, woodwork and flooring always work well. Any strong color can then be added as accents with rugs and accessories. These items can easily be changed to give a neutral color scheme a new look later on.

LINKING – WITH FLOORING

Visual continuity and a feeling of space can be achieved by using the same or similar color floorings throughout a home. Your choice of floorcoverings do not all have to be exactly the same material or color to produce an effect of continuity. For instance, a honey or tan mini-print carpet in the hall and on the stairs works well with, perhaps, slightly darker floor tiles in the kitchen and a toning plain caramel carpet or stripped floorboards in the living room.

Again, when it comes to floorcoverings for the whole house, neutral colors such as beige, gray and cream work very successfully because they allow a wide choice of decoration. Choosing a light shade for a floorcovering was once considered hopelessly impractical, but with some of today's new materials this no longer applies. Modern off-white and cream textured vinyls, for example, can be extremely hardwearing and perfect for brightening a dark hallway or kitchen.

A few well-chosen rugs in similar patterns and colors can also link different flooring areas throughout a home by leading the eye through. Oriental rugs in rich colors, dhurries in pastel shades, or strong geometric art deco design rugs in neutral colors can usually echo and link colors in several room schemes.

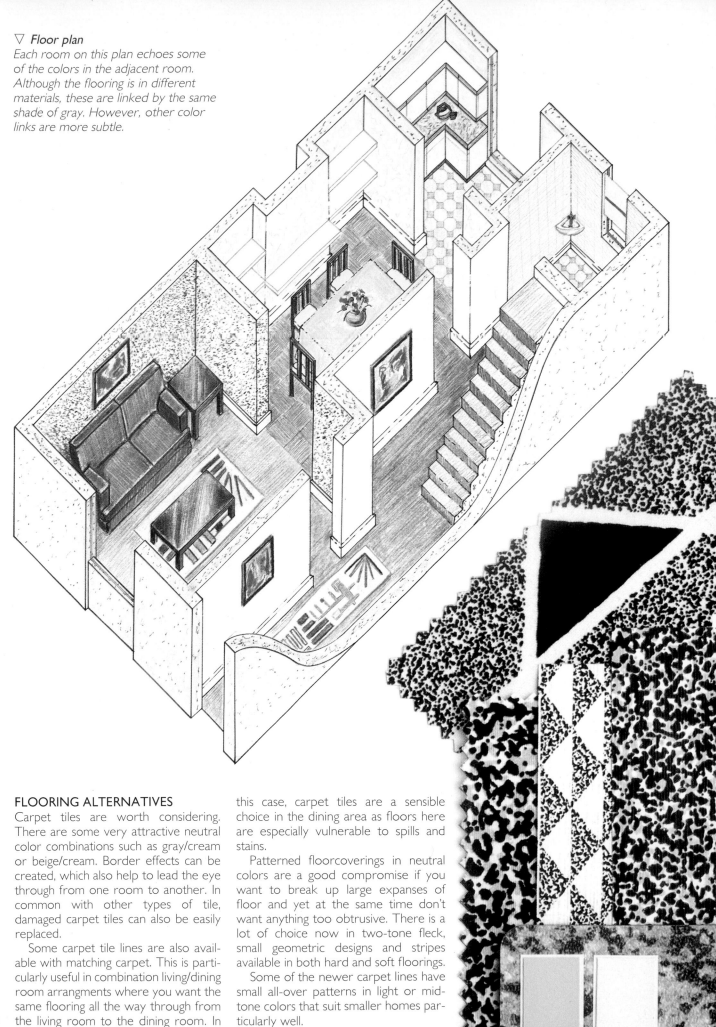

▽ *Floor plan*
Each room on this plan echoes some of the colors in the adjacent room. Although the flooring is in different materials, these are linked by the same shade of gray. However, other color links are more subtle.

FLOORING ALTERNATIVES

Carpet tiles are worth considering. There are some very attractive neutral color combinations such as gray/cream or beige/cream. Border effects can be created, which also help to lead the eye through from one room to another. In common with other types of tile, damaged carpet tiles can also be easily replaced.

Some carpet tile lines are also available with matching carpet. This is particularly useful in combination living/dining room arrangments where you want the same flooring all the way through from the living room to the dining room. In

this case, carpet tiles are a sensible choice in the dining area as floors here are especially vulnerable to spills and stains.

Patterned floorcoverings in neutral colors are a good compromise if you want to break up large expanses of floor and yet at the same time don't want anything too obtrusive. There is a lot of choice now in two-tone fleck, small geometric designs and stripes available in both hard and soft floorings.

Some of the newer carpet lines have small all-over patterns in light or mid-tone colors that suit smaller homes particularly well.

FLOORING THRESHOLDS

There is one unfortunate snag with the brass and aluminium carpet threshold plates that hold the carpet edges firmly in place in doorways: they can detract from the overall feeling of continuity. There are wooden threshold plates that suit some interior schemes and are also less obtrusive. These can be stained, polished or painted to blend exactly with a floorcovering.

LINKING – WITH WALL COLORS AND ACCENTS

The simplest way to handle all the different colors in rooms that lead off a hall or landing is to pick several different shades of the same color. In this way they harmonize without appearing bland.

First, decide on the mood and whether you want it warm or cool. Magnolia, maize and deep egg-yolk yellow in rooms off a pale cream-painted hall or landing work well together and achieve a warm effect. Pale blues, grays and lavender, on the other hand, would create a much softer, cooler feeling.

Accents in pictures, lighting and accessories also help lead the eye from one room into another. The eye will focus on any brilliant, primary colored accents in an all-neutral scheme.

For instance, a slight touch of red in the framed print of the black and white living room opposite has been repeated in the framed prints in the hallway, red flowers on the dining room table and kitchen accessories.

Small touches of red are also echoed in the red enameled faucets and striped blind.

▽ *Fabrics, wallcoverings and carpet*
These fabrics and coordinating wallcoverings were the spark for the whole downstairs color scheme. A mid-gray carpet is a practical 'through' color, while touches of bright red in accessories and pictures lead the eye through to the dining area and kitchen.

△ *Dramatic black and white*
Inspired by the wallcoverings and fabrics of the living room, the whole house has been planned from this black and white theme leading through to sunny yellows, creams and turquoise. A mid-gray flooring is a good versatile color that can take a wide range of accents.

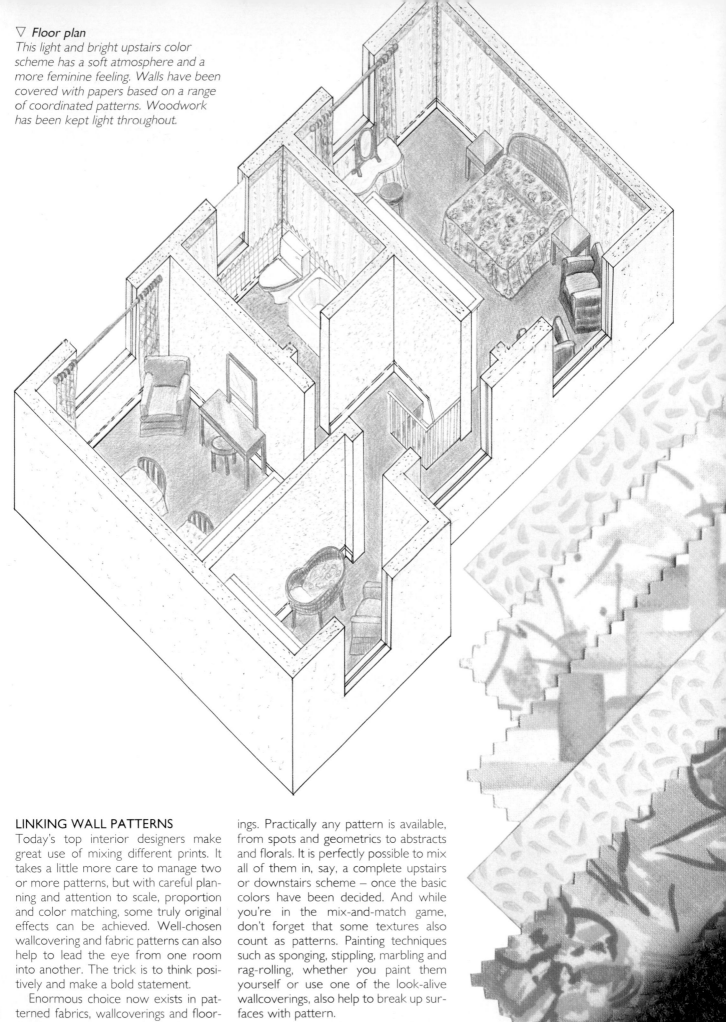

This light and bright upstairs color
scheme has a soft atmosphere and a
more feminine feeling. Walls have been
covered with papers based on a range
of coordinated patterns. Woodwork
has been kept light throughout.

LINKING WALL PATTERNS

Today's top interior designers make
great use of mixing different prints. It
takes a little more care to manage two
or more patterns, but with careful planning and attention to scale, proportion
and color matching, some truly original
effects can be achieved. Well-chosen
wallcovering and fabric patterns can also
help to lead the eye from one room
into another. The trick is to think posi-
tively and make a bold statement.

Enormous choice now exists in patterned fabrics, wallcoverings and floorings. Practically any pattern is available,
from spots and geometrics to abstracts
and florals. It is perfectly possible to mix
all of them in, say, a complete upstairs
or downstairs scheme – once the basic
colors have been decided. And while
you're in the mix-and-match game,
don't forget that some textures also
count as patterns. Painting techniques
such as sponging, stippling, marbling and
rag-rolling, whether you paint them
yourself or use one of the look-alive
wallcoverings, also help to break up surfaces with pattern.

SCHEMING WITH PATTERNS

Patterns can make large rooms feel cozier but too many in a small room can be claustrophobic. An interesting border with complementary paper and fabric is more effective.

When color scheming for adjoining rooms, first choose a pattern. In this case, the bathroom wallcovering and border inspired the whole upstairs color scheme. It is a good idea to isolate the colors in the most dominant pattern and build your color scheme based upon these. Work in natural daylight as it is difficult to achieve good results in artificial light.

The four rooms and landing in the floor plan opposite are all color-schemed using a number of coordinating wallcoverings and borders. The apricot and blue in the bathroom border, for instance, are picked up in the spare bedroom's apricot and blue floral wallcoverings and fabric. A muted green carpet echoes greens in the border.

△ *Rosebud stripe*
This bathroom with coordinated wallcovering, border and tiles inspired the entire upstairs color scheme. All the elements are shown in the sample board below.

COLOR INSPIRATION

When visualizing a hall or landing color scheme, it helps to leave all the doors leading to the adjoining rooms open. You can then see how the hallway and landing walls act as a 'frame' for the rooms. For a warmer scheme the walls in the hallway would look equally good in a solid maroon. The molding, painted white to stand out, could remain white as a nice contrast against the maroon walls and dark wood floor. The addition of Oriental scatter rugs could have a colorful yet softening effect. Other patterns could work too, as long as they remain within the color scheme.

Where woodwork is changing color from one room to the next you are faced with painting two sides of a door in different colors. Care needs to be taken in deciding exactly where one color should end and the other begin. When a door is closed all is well, but when it is open you'll see the edges as well. It's best to paint the opening edge of the door the same color as the face that opens into the room and the hinged edge to match the other face. This way, when the door is left open, the color of the visible edge and the face of the door are continuous from whichever room they are viewed.

▽ *Victorian decor*
Different wallcovering patterns in the hallway and bedroom can create a unified look if the color scheme is the same and the patterns are compatible.

HANDLING SAMPLES SUCCESSFULLY

Samples – and a well-planned sample board – are the key to working out a color scheme that turns out the way you want.

The prospect of putting a room scheme together – choosing colors for walls, curtains, floor and wallcoverings – is exciting. But with so many possibilites to choose from it's hard to know where to start.

That's where samples come in. By collecting a variety of samples – a mixture of plains, patterns and textures, wallcoverings, paint charts, carpets and fabrics – you can make sure the color scheme is successful.

First you need a starting point of some kind. It could be a sofa, carpet or some curtains you have already, or perhaps just an idea of the effect you want – warm and lively, for instance, or calm and harmonious. The color wheel (see The Language of Color, page 13) is a useful tool to help you identify the colors that work with your sofa or carpet, or that create the effect you're after.

Play with the samples in different groupings. Once you have decided what goes well together take it a step further and make up a sample board like interior designers do. This way, all the swatches of fabric, wallcoverings, carpet and paint can be seen together in roughly the proportions they will be used. Then you can start to see in your mind's eye what the finished room will look like.

Finally, allow time for decisions. Impulse buys are usually the ones you regret later. Keep the sample board in the room for a few days to see how you feel about each element after the first flush of enthusiasm wears off.

◁ *Patterns*
There is an enormous choice available – floral and geometric, abstract and traditional. Small patterns may lose definition in a large room, while big patterns can overpower a small room.

◁ *Solids*
Solid paint, carpets or fabrics, such as cottons and velvets, help to set off patterns and textures.

▷ *Textures*
Texture describes how a material appeals to the sense of touch – rough or smooth, ribbed or velvety. Fabrics and wallcoverings are also printed to look like textures – spattered, wood grain, watered silk and other tactile effects.

PLANNING AROUND A PATTERN

The starting point can be any existing pattern on a sofa, a carpet, curtains, wallcovering, even a cushion. This will provide the basis for your color scheme – and your collection of samples.

Begin by identifying the different colors in the pattern and then select two or three to become the basis for the scheme.

Collect the samples in a variety of solids, patterns and textures, so you have plenty of choice. Solids do not always provide enough visual interest and patterns can sometimes be too much, so it's important to consider textures too.

Collecting the samples It is always better to choose from samples of the actual items – a square of carpet, for example, or a swatch of fabric – rather than from printed images in catalogues that may be different colors from the real thing. If you are designing a room around beiges, for instance, a carpet that turns out slightly pinker than the printed sample could spoil the whole

color scheme.

Handling patterns It is always difficult to imagine what a finished scheme will look like on the basis of tiny samples. So with large-patterned wallcoverings or fabric, try to get a large sample.

Look at the photos in pattern books to help you imagine the overall effect and whether, in quantity, it will be pleasing or overbearing. If in doubt, it's better to buy one roll first rather than put up with long-term disappointment.

Handling paint In the same way, it is difficult to imagine what a whole room painted in a color chosen from a paint chart will look like. You need to see the color on its own, not as a tiny patch surrounded by other similar colors.

Once you've narrowed your choice down to one or two colors, it's a good idea to buy a small sample of each and try them out in the room – but remember that wet paint usually dries a shade or two darker. Paint onto a large sheet of cardboard to see how the color looks next to different pieces of furniture, in the sun, or in a dark corner.

▽ **The starting point**
The sofa fabric makes a good base for the scheme because it contains so many colors.

▷ **Solids**
Identify the colors in the sofa fabric and collect samples of them – floor coverings and paint charts, fabrics and wallcoverings.

▽ **Patterns**
The sofa fabric has a distinctive pattern, so choose other patterns that include the same colors. Check that pattern scales work together.

▽ **Textures**
Choose textured materials in similar colors for surface interest.

MAKING A SAMPLE BOARD

A sample board is one of the 'tricks of the trade' of professional interior designers. It helps you judge whether colors, patterns and textures work together, and gives a good idea how the scheme will look.

To make a sample board you need a piece of plain cardboard about 8in. × 12in. as a base (a piece of oak tag will do, but keep the color of the board neutral).

Usually about one-sixth of the color in a room comes from the floor, another sixth from curtains and upholstery, and the remaining two-thirds from walls and ceiling. Try to aim for samples in these proportions so they virtually cover the board – if necessary, get two or three samples of the chosen carpet to make a large enough patch. If the floor is wood, see if you can find something to match.

Finally, try out bits of wool or paint chips to see which accents work best with the overall color scheme.

Using the sample board
Left: the sample board. Below: how the room will eventually look.

BRIGHT IDEA

PATTERN HINTS

One problem in choosing a patterned wallcovering or fabric (particularly one with a large design) is imagining how it will look when it is hung. Some pattern books have photographs that show the overall effect in a room; and some shops provide a large 'viewing' mirror – an idea you can copy at home.

If you stand back and hold up the sample in front of the mirror the distance between you and the mirror is doubled in the reflection, giving you a more objective view of how the sample will look. Some small patterns seem to 'disappear' or merge into a single color when viewed at a distance.

To get an idea of the repeat effect, hold the sample at right angles close to the mirror: the pattern is reflected and appears twice as wide.

SHOPPING HINTS

It's worth exploring specialty furniture shops to look at pattern books with well coordinated lines of wallcoverings and fabrics. Even if you don't buy them, they provide ideas for what colors go together and how to mix patterns and solids.

For a small fee, some shops will supply larger samples. Or, for a returnable deposit, they will loan out a sample.

THE IMPORTANCE OF LIGHTING

When choosing paints and materials, it is essential to make your selection under the same lighting conditions as those in your home – another reason why collecting samples is a good idea. You should take the samples into the room to be decorated and look at them by both daylight and by electric light at night. Consider when you use the room most. If it's during the daytime, then make sure you choose your scheme from the samples that look best in daylight. Think about the atmosphere you want to create, too – a warm, inviting living room or a fresh, sunny bedroom, for example.

It is easy to think that all electric lights are the same. In fact, the various types of artificial lighting affect certain colors in different ways. A normal incandescent light (the kind produced by standard light bulbs) makes pale blues slightly dull and gray, while reds appear more vivid. Under a warm light fluorescent strip, purples have distinctly pink overtones, but pinks appear dull.

Colors can vary in daylight conditions too. If you look around a room by day, you'll notice how the light on one wall is slightly different from that on the wall next to it – the intensity of light depends on the position of the windows and doors, the direction the house faces and the time of day.

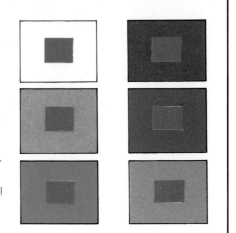

HOW COLORS AFFECT ONE ANOTHER

The red used here is the same in every illustration. See how different it looks when it's placed next to other colors.

☐ White makes it look clear and intense, black makes it lighter.

☐ Gray makes the red darker, blue makes it brighter.

☐ Next to orange – a closely related color – the red looks darker and less true; green – the color directly opposite on the color wheel – makes red appear very bright.

ONE SOLID COLOR – THREE DIFFERENT LOOKS

If you're starting with a solid color – whether it's walls, carpet or upholstery – you have an almost limitless choice. So think about the kind of look you want to create – it could be elegant or country, flowery or high-tech – and then choose with that in mind.

In the room schemes below, the basic starting point is the toffee-colored carpet. By mixing patterns and textures, and branching out with loosely coordi-

nated colors and patterns, it is possible to create three schemes, each with a totally different feel.

The overall look of a room depends not just on colors, but also on the size and type of patterns – anything from large floral prints to small geometrical designs – and the textures of the materials used. So consider these different factors as you go about collecting samples.

△ *Elegant and understated*
The subtle 'textured' patterns used in the fabric and wallcovering echo the carpet texture. The colors all relate to one another, and are colors found in nature, calm and subdued. The curtains and sofa are chosen for their understated, elegant lines, and the overall effect is lightness.

△ Sophisticated fun

Here pattern is combined with pattern, spots with stripes, stripes with florals for a spontaneous and freestyle look. It works because the colors are slightly muted but still lively, the patterns abstract, the textures smooth. A touch of toffee in the fabrics is just enough to unify the scheme.

△ Cottage effect

Here, common denominator colors of sand, toffee and maroon make patterns of different scales and character work together. Sand-colored cushions and piping break up the large area of maroon on the sofa, while the smooth wall surface offsets the woven cotton of the sofa fabric and the twist pile texture of the carpet.

SAME SAMPLES – TWO SCHEMES

Exactly the same materials can be used to create quite different effects, depending on how you use larger and smaller patterns, lighter and darker colors.

If you can find a picture of a room like the one to be decorated, it's worth tracing it onto plain paper and coloring in the different areas to match the samples. This gives an idea of how a large area of china blue on walls, for example, will look as opposed to a much smaller area of the same blue used for blinds or a cushion.

▷ *Light and airy*
The bold 'stencil-look' wallpaper pattern creates a fresh airy look. Patterns with white backgrounds usually make rooms seem light and more spacious.

▷ *Rich and glowing*
For an all-over color effect, the floral mini-print wallpaper is used. Note how the background blue predominates: colored grounds tend to hold furnishings together, bring walls in.

HARMONIOUS COLORS

Combine closely related colors to create harmonious schemes that are easy to live with.

Greens, blues and mauves work well together; pinks, peaches and apricots are a successful mixture, too. When you combine colors like these, which are closely related on the color wheel, you can be certain of creating harmonious color schemes.

The degree of harmony depends on how closely related the colors are. The color wheel that appears on page 13 is divided into 12 sections but it could be divided into many more, with subtler differences in color.

If you move around the color wheel and choose any group of colors that lie near (but not necessarily adjacent to) each other, they will create a comfortable harmony. The most obvious way to divide colors is into warm and cool groups. Pinks, reds and yellows, for example, are all on the warm side; blues, green and mauves are on the cool side. A warm harmony of colors creates an inviting atmosphere in a large or small room; and a careful combination of cool colors can create space.

TEMPERATES

You can also make successful harmonies by mixing colors that link the warm and the cool side of the color wheel. These are called temperate color combinations. Orange, yellow and green, for example, are a warm temperate harmony mixing warm colors (orange and yellow) with a touch of coolness (green). Red and pink with mauve are a warm temperate combination from the other end of the range.

Yellow used with green and blue, or blue and mauve with pink, are both cool temperate color combinations in which cool colors are warmed up with a color from the warm side of the wheel. So, if your starting point is blue – maybe in the carpet or on the walls – and you want a harmonious scheme you can move in either direction on the color wheel, towards a sunny yellow or a warm pink.

Harmony is even easier to create using tints and shades of just one color – think of the hundreds of shades there are of any single color. However, this kind of scheme often lacks life, so additions of small accents of strong or more contrasting colors, and varying textures, help to make the overall scheme more interesting.

Natural harmony
Warm and cool harmonies are found in the subtle colors in nature – yellows, oranges, russets, ochres, reds and pinks; or soft blue, lilac, mauve, greens and purples.

WARM HARMONIES

Using a harmony of warm colors always makes a room appear inviting and comfortable. The warm range of colors stretches from scarlet through oranges, to yellow, and includes pinks, pale peaches, rich plums and ochres.

The closer a color is to a primary such as red – the warmest and most vibrant of the warm range – the more intense the color will be. These intense versions of warm colors are very lively and need to be carefully controlled, otherwise they can be very difficult to live with.

So, if you want to avoid a restless combination of colors, choose a harmonious scheme. Pick colors that are close together on the color wheel, mixing pure colors with lighter and darker tones.

Remember that the strength of colors varies. The richness of autumn can be found in the darker versions of oranges and red; the pastel equivalents are softer and fresher, and probably better suited to warming up a small cold room without being overbearing.

In this living room the apricot walls, scorched pink velvet upholstery and peach lamp shade give it a warm, comfortable feel – with such a high ceiling it could easily have turned out cold and austere.

△ **Warm and welcoming**
A warm harmony of colors in this large living room are perfectly complemented by the rich gilt of the mirror frame and the natural wood of the table and the fireplace.

◁ **Oranges and lemons**
Yellow is a particularly useful temperate color. It can be a warm sunny yellow with a hint of orange, or a cooler lemon, closer to green. It is also easily influenced by other colors.

   The warm yellow in this room is tempered by the apricot and soft green in the floral print of the upholstery and the blinds.

◁ **Hot pinks, cool lilacs**
Pinks from the warm range of colors are cooled with a lilac-gray in this color scheme. The warm coral pink is mixed with a vivid pink in the upholstery fabric and the blind. The lilac walls and the pale pink of the painted wicker chair blend with the lilac-gray carpet and the gray table.

COOL HARMONY

Blue sky and green grass — a harmonious color scheme made in heaven. Almost any shade of blue goes with all the different greens — light blues with emerald, soft green with soft turquoise, mauve with deep green.

Interesting cool harmonies are simply created using different amounts of several colors and by using different intensities of color.

In the light airy bedroom above, for instance, a combination of blues with pale green creates a serene, restful atmosphere — refreshing to wake up to. The pale moss green and the lilac-gray of the carpet soften the cool crispness of the overall scheme.

In a color scheme that is predominantly blue it seems quite natural to add a little green, a closely related cool color, to lighten the effect.

COOL TEMPERATES

It is often a good idea to introduce a touch of warmth to the cools. In a scheme dominated by mauve, using deep pink, a warm color close to mauve on the color wheel, will maintain the harmonious effect and add warmth and interest.

Similarly, at the green end of the cool range, a warm color such as a sandy beige, could be included — in cushion or curtain fabrics, perhaps — to warm up an otherwise cool scheme.

△ *Cool companions*
In this bedroom, which gets plenty of natural light and warmth, a combination of soft blue, mint green and lilac-gray creates a very fresh atmosphere.

◁ Cool alternatives

Colors from the other end of the cool range – blues and greens - are combined here with a soft, sandy yellow. The coolness of the blues and greens are equally balanced; although the green appears in smaller areas it is more intense. The element of warmth in the yellowish beige softens an otherwise cool scheme and adds to the airiness of the room.

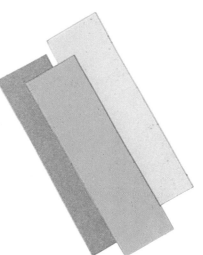

◁ Grays and pinks

Here a cool harmony of blue-gray lilac is combined with deep pink.

The walls below the chair rail are painted in a delicate lilac; above the rail a soft pink is sponged over white. The matching curtain and tablecloth fabric combines a broad blue-gray stripe with splashes of vivid pink, repeated in the hydrangea blooms outside.

White is used to bring light and freshness into the overall scheme.

SINGLE HARMONY

Combining shades of just one color is an alternative way of creating a harmonious color scheme. Any color you choose will have a wide range of tints and shades from the palest and freshest to the very darkest. A restful combination of greens, for instance, can include a pale jade and a deep green.

It's important to choose tones from all parts of the range so that the color scheme works. Using a selection of shades from the dark and the light ends of the range tends to make the overall effect seem disjointed, because there are no mid-tones.

Once you've decided on the color, it's quite simple to put together a single color scheme, but it's also easy for these schemes to turn out to be monotonous. To avoid ending up with a dull lifeless room, add accents of color in cushions or vases perhaps.

The accent color need not be strong. However, they are most effective when they are contrast colors chosen from the opposite side of the color wheel – red or orange with green, perhaps, or blue with yellow – but be careful not to break up the harmony by using too many.

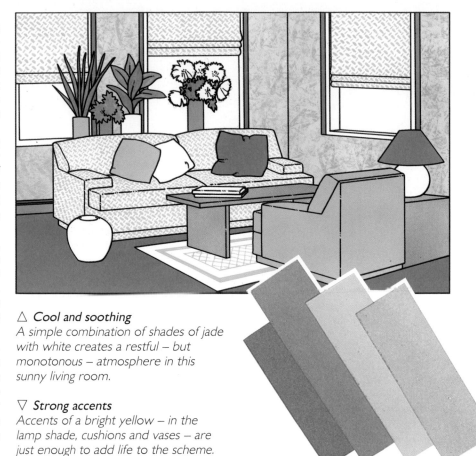

△ *Cool and soothing*
A simple combination of shades of jade with white creates a restful – but monotonous – atmosphere in this sunny living room.

▽ *Strong accents*
Accents of a bright yellow – in the lamp shade, cushions and vases – are just enough to add life to the scheme.

WORKING WITH ACCENT COLORS

Learn how to use touches of color — warm or cool, subtle or bright — to bring new life to your color schemes.

Most color schemes are improved by the addition of accents — the final touches of color that can make a room come alive, or complement a color scheme. They are usually provided by accessories, such as lamp shades, cushions, picture frames, towels, soaps, tablecloths, candles, flowers, or blinds. Using accents successfully is simple once you understand a few basic rules.

USING ACCENTS

The power of an accent color depends on the background of colors it is combined with. If, for example, the color scheme is dominated by a warm sandy yellow, the accent color could come from the cool side of the color wheel — blues or greens, perhaps- to introduce a lively contrast; a choice of red or pink accents — almost opposite yellow on the color wheel — would be more striking.

Accents needn't be strong contrast colors to be successful. Adding accents that are closely related to the basic color scheme has a harmonious and restful effect, and can be used to emphasize individual tones.

Don't put off using accents if there is pattern in the room. A color that is common to all the patterns can be picked out as an accent to provide a visual link between the various elements. A soft pastel floral wallcovering in pinks and greens combined with a plain striped sofa in a shade of green, for instance, would be perfectly complemented by a few accents in a more intense tone of the same green.

Try to avoid using the same accent color in too many places, or too many accent colors in one room. In a living room, for example, limit the accents to three or four places, such as cushions, a lamp shade or a picture frame that can be easily changed.

NEUTRAL COLOR SCHEMES

Accents are particularly important in monochromatic or neutral color schemes, which can sometimes look dull. Try covering up the shocking pink accents in the picture on this page and see how the well-balanced neutral color scheme of gray and white loses its impact.

Neutral color schemes can provide a background for a mixture of different accent colors. The combination can be harmonious or contrasting depending on the effect you want to create.

Color power
This strong and plain neutral color scheme needs splashes of a powerful color, such as a bright vivid pink, to bring it alive.

CHOOSING YOUR ACCENTS

Look carefully at the contents of the room before deciding on accent colors. Upholstery fabric, paintings, posters or china are already part of the decoration scheme and often provide the inspiration. Accents are easy to change and a familiar color can be quickly given a fresh look with a new range of accents.

▷ *Quick change*
Changing a tablecloth is an easy way to bring fresh color into an eating area. Match the color scheme by using a color found on the wallcovering.

▽ *Perfect link*
The strong red of the wallcovering is accented on the lamp shades and the nightstand cover, the piping of the draperies and canopy. It is also repeated throughout the fabric patterns on the comforter, chairs, and dust ruffles, adding zest to an otherwise plainly colored room.

△ **Painted inspiration**
The accent colors used for the cushions in this living room are taken from the painting on the left-hand wall. The cream walls and furniture provide a neutral background that can, therefore, take more accent colors than a colored room. Here five different accents are used – pink, red, green, yellow and blue – any more and the effect would be spotty. The deep blue vases on the mantelpiece echoes the painting over the fireplace.

▷ **Blue and white**
In this bedroom, white was picked out of the painting on the wall and used as the accent color for the wall lights, baseboard and traditional fireplace mantel. It makes a strong, crisp contrast with the cool blue color scheme.

Picking out the architectural features, such as cornice, baseboards, ceiling rose, molding on paneled doors or fireplace mantel is another way of bringing accents into a decorating scheme.

CONTRAST AND HARMONY

Contrasting accent colors can have a variety of effects on a color scheme, from the strongest impact created by bringing together opposites on the color wheel – a bright red used in a green room scheme, for instance, to subtle mixtures of pastel tones.

Harmonious accent colors are easier to use successfully. They should be close to the basic color scheme on the color wheel but they can be darker or lighter depending on the effect you want to create.

△ *Warm contrast*
The rich deep red in the floral curtain fabric has been picked up as a strong contrasting accent color in the matting on the pictures, lamp shade and cushion in this warm yellow living room.

▷ *Sharp accents*
Neutral color schemes can take almost any color as an accent. The sink, cabinet handles, window blind and matching accessories have been added in bright red to liven up this stark white room.

△ **Cool harmony**
You can add interest to a harmonious color scheme – without destroying the harmonious effect – by using stronger or lighter versions of the same or closely-related colors. In this cool blue and green living room, the lamp shade in jade emphasizes the more delicate tones of the marbled wallcovering and the sofa fabric.

▷ **Country colors**
In this living room the color scheme is based on the colors in the floral upholstery fabric – soft moss green, beige and pale blue. The coffee tables are painted in a deeper shade of blue to add interest without destroying the harmonious effect. A deep green would make a good alternative accent.

USING ACCENTS WITH NEUTRALS

Neutral colors include any shade of gray in the range of tones from white to black, as well as beiges, browns, cream and ochres. Neutral color schemes can easily become dull and lifeless without accents; but almost any color can be used as an accent and, to change the mood completely, simply change the accessories. In this beige scheme a variety of contrasting and harmonious accents has been added.

△ The fine black lines of the picture frames, the lamp bases and the trim on the bedcover and cushion work well as a strong neutral accent in this bland color scheme.

△ A group of drawings in deep terra-cotta frames set against a cream marbled wall, with matching lamp shades and piping on the cushions, add a warm touch.

△ A neutral color scheme should include a range of textures and accents to add visual interest. Touches of bright color such as yellow liven up this scheme.

CONTRASTING COLOR SCHEMES

Room schemes made up from contrasting colors can be strong and eye-catching or gently colored and restful.

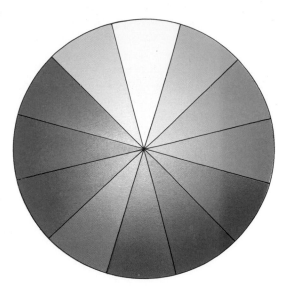

Contrasting color schemes, whether in bright or pastel tones, have one thing in common: their principal colors lie on opposite sides of the color wheel.

They do not necessarily have to be direct opposites, but can be taken from anywhere on the opposing half of the color wheel: with red as the parent color, any color from indigo to yellow ochre can be used as a contrast, or with leaf green as the parent, any shade from orange through red, pink, and violet can be used. Tonal values are important as the two main colors need to be fairly evenly balanced. The less intense the

shade you choose, the easier the scheme will become: both pastel and muted shades, even when contrasting, in the end become harmonious.

Balance is important. Don't use two colors in equal quantities as they can 'intensify' each other. On the other hand, avoid the spotty effect created by just dotting the complementary color around the scheme. At the same time, using just two colors can be somber, so use others to act as background and accents to give the room a 'lift.' They can make the main colors more vibrant or tone them down.

△ **Graded color wheel** shows all the hues, from deep tones to light pastels.

▽ **Confident contrast**
The boldest of colors and patterns were used confidently to decorate this interior. A colorful Oriental theme adds interest to this already vivacious setting.

◁ *Clearly contrasting*
The parent color – yellow – contrasts in classic fashion with clear sky blue. The yellow is present in two hues: soft and daffodil painted on the table and baseboards, sharp buttercup as accent in the teapot, cup and saucer. The creamy-beige wall and blue-beige carpet tie the colors together.

▽ *Contrast – or harmony?*
Pale pastel-yellow walls inset with cream panels act as the parent color in this elegant room. A clear delft blue in the screen, tablecloths and cushions acts as a contrast. The creamy-gray carpet and upholstery form the neutral backdrop, with yellow piping and ribbons as accent. Light entering the room from the window makes the two sofas appear almost different in color as it falls on them. The mix of pastels, while strictly complementary, is almost harmonious because they are so light in tone.

IMPORTANCE OF LIGHT

It is important to look at the colors in the room where they are to be used, as different light can affect coloring to a considerable degree.

If you want to use a strong color for the walls, it is worthwhile buying a small sample of paint and painting a large sheet of cardboard. Prop it against the wall for a few days to see the effect of different light conditions in your room. Strong colors tend to look even stronger on a large area and in a small room the color reflects from one wall to the other to intensify the effect.

Lay color samples against each other while you consider them, not against white or a neutral, and don't put more than three intense colors together. On the other hand, if you are using muted or pastel shades, you can mix any number of colors. Use pattern – in carpet, for example – to link the parent color with complementaries.

▷ *Classic contrast*

Dark rooms with little light can take more intense colors in a contrast color scheme because they become more muted. In this bedroom a very strong yellow – which might be overpowering in a lighter room – is used as the contrast color against a mid-blue parent. The darker blue stencil designs on the wall and frills on the quilt, with white lamp shades and frills on the canopy, act as accents. On the floor, the rug combines all the colors used and the coffee-colored carpet acts as a neutral background.

▽ *Color ranges*

A range of blue and yellow paint swatches show how well these two opposing colors work together in contrasting schemes.

△ *Geometric contrast*
Turquoise-painted walls and deeper-toned carpet form an all-enveloping parent color contrasted by angular blocks of pink. A deeper-toned pink highlights the woodwork. Subtle indirect lighting hidden behind the headboard creates interesting light-and-shadow effects on the wall above. Bed linen in the palest of pastel pinks forms the neutral relief color.

◁ *Three-way contrast*
Three blocks of color in almost equal weight make an exciting modern scheme in a café-style dining corner. While the yellow and turquoise are nearly the same tonal value, the deep red floor is altogether much darker. The same red, used with light navy blue, serves as accent color in the painted border around the wall. The neutral shiny black table and chairs make the colors appear brighter.

CONTRAST COLOR CHART

COLOR	CONTRAST	ACCENTS	NEUTRALS
RED Scarlet Terra-cotta	Emerald Dark ivy French navy Bright blue	Tan / Sand Naples Yellow / Dusky pink	Cream / White Ivory / Beige
GREEN Deep blue-green Citrus green	Peach Deep dusky pink Royal blue	Light green / Turquoise Purple / Lilac	Oyster / White Silver / White
YELLOW	Mid-blue	Green	Yellowish white / Green-grays
BLUE	Burnt orange	Scarlet	Blue-white / Gray
PINK	Turquoise	Deep blue-green	Magnolia / Blue-gray

BRIGHT IDEA

Work out a scheme You can work out an interesting contrasting color scheme by using the standard color wheel.

Trace over the diagram at right, then retrace it onto cardboard or thick paper. (Alternatively, use carbon paper to mark the diagram on to a sheet of paper underneath.) Cut out the shaded segments and pin the circle through the marked center point onto the color wheel printed on page 43.

The triangular segment represents the parent color. Turn the circle around on the wheel, depending on which color you are planning to use as the parent, and any of the colors showing through the semi-circle window can be used as a contrast.

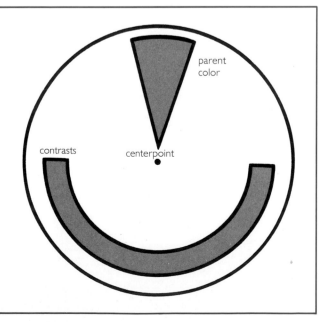

EXPERIMENT WITH COLOR

If you're not totally color confident, it is sometimes a good idea to experiment with color scheming in a smaller room, or by using paints – which are inexpensive and easy to change if you are unhappy with the results.

A bathroom, half bath, or powder room (all too often unexcitingly decorated) are good places to start. You may hit upon a color scheme that pleases you, but if not, the walls can be quickly repainted. Try using lighter or more muted shades. Don't forget to include calming neutrals and a few accent points to obtain the complete effect.

This sort of experimentation helps to build up your confidence and enables you to create a really exciting color scheme in the future in one of the main rooms of your home.

△ *Holly inspiration*
The classic contrast of red and green, used here in mid-tones, gives this bathroom a cheerful aspect. Neutral white on the ceiling and painted beams add lightness and brightness.

▽ *Variations on a theme*
This bathroom with butterscotch walls contrasted by a lilac-colored bath provides an interesting variation on a yellow-and-blue theme. The grayish-green lavatory and tiles provide gentle accent color, with white as the background neutral.

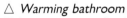

△ *Warming bathroom*
Rich terra-cotta walls give a warming glow, contrasted by the vibrant blue-painted bath exterior. Gleaming brass faucets act as accents and the neutral white ceiling lightens the whole room.

UNDERSTANDING TONE

If you can't put your finger on what is missing from a room scheme – it's often the tonal mix that is wrong.

Basically, 'tone' describes the lightness and darkness of a color. Technically, the tone of a color can be affected by two things: the *intensity* (amount) of the color and *value* – the amount of black or white it contains. The combination of intensity and value produces the *tone*.

Whether you like muted or pastel shades, warm colors or bright contrasts, understanding tone really does help in making decisions about colors. It also helps you to create a well-balanced scheme which is neither too bland and boring, nor too busy.

An all-over, one-color scheme can be made visually interesting by using several different tones of that color – from the palest pastel through to a really deep shade. Alternatively, a many-colored, many-patterned room – which might seem in danger of becoming a visual mess – can be saved if all the colors are closely related in tone. And when evaluating the overall tonal mix don't forget to take the tone of any woodwork into account.

To use tone successfully, it helps if you can recognize similar tones in different colors – something you are probably already doing subconsciously. Once you do understand tonal intensity and values, and how to combine them, you can create room schemes that are lively and interesting as well as satisfactorily balanced.

How tone works It is often hard to notice the tonal relationship of colors when looking at a colored photograph, but in a black-and-white photograph or a film, where colors are converted into shades of gray, it is much more obvious. Good newspaper pictures and old 1940s films work because there's a good range of tonal contrast. The two photographs of the same room below – first in color, then in black-and-white – clearly show the different tonal values.

◁ *Balancing the tones*
The cheerful, multi-colored patchwork blends harmoniously because many of the patches are of approximately the same tonal value; only the darker blue and white are different. Looking at the black-and-white photograph you'll notice how the darker blue tone ties in with the wood fireplace and that without the white patches the overall effect would be quite dull and lifeless.

49

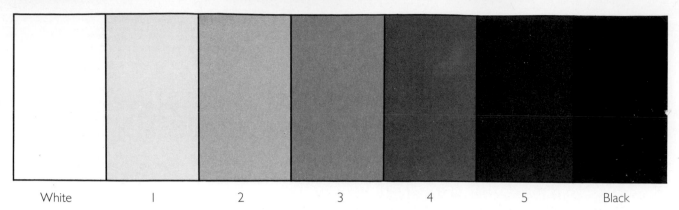

White	1	2	3	4	5	Black

TONE SCALE

The diagram above shows seven gradations of tone ranged between pure white and pure black. The tones range from very light to a semi-light, quite light, mid-tone, quite dark to very dark. This is a simplified tone scale, and is one that can be easily distinguished by the human eye. Your eye can quickly learn to give an approximate 1-5 rating to different colors.

Below is a range of shades in three colors progressing from the lightest shade to the darkest. Comparing the colors in a line across the page you'll notice that each shade has roughly the same tonal value or intensity.

HOW TO TEST FOR TONE

To consider the tones that are contained in a fabric design you are thinking of using, here is an experiment to try.

☐ First, match paint samples as closely as possible to the colors in the fabric.

☐ Next, cut them out and then lay them out on an off-white background such as a gray or buff envelope.

☐ Then squint a little at the colors. Move them around if necessary, so that they lie next to other shades.

☐ Squint again; if the colors seem to merge, then they are quite close together in tone. On the other hand, if they don't merge, then the colors are of different tones.

☐ Armed with this knowledge, you will be able to make much more effective decisions when choosing the shades and tones of any accent colors you want to accompany your decorating scheme and to enhance to the maximum effect.

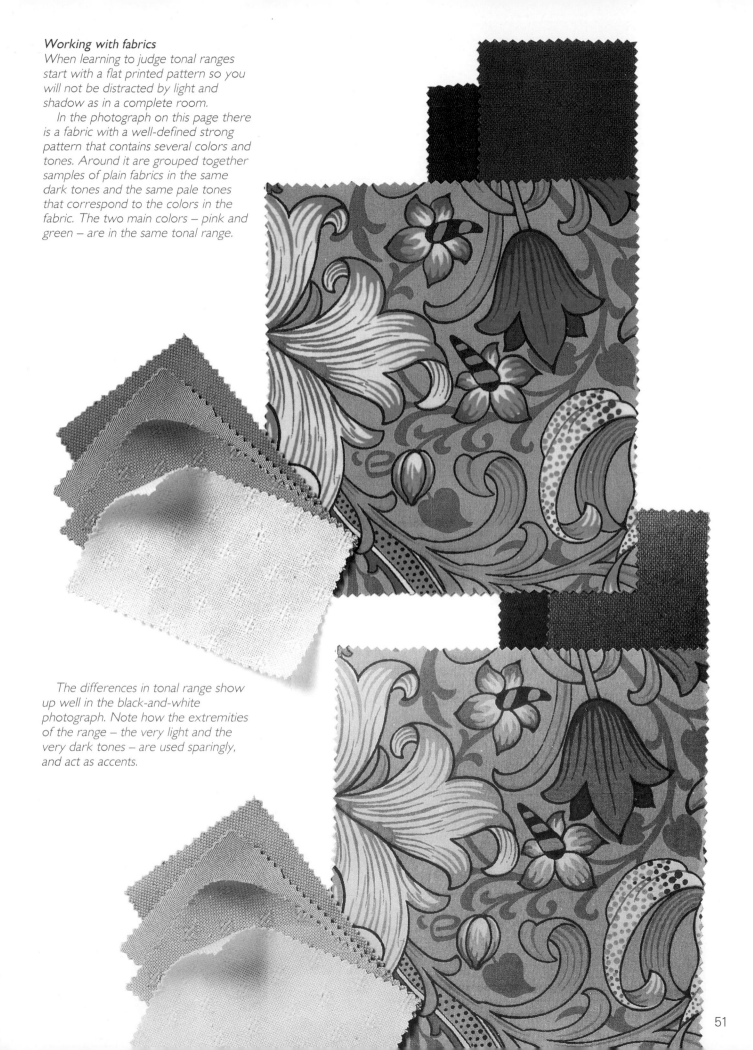

Working with fabrics

When learning to judge tonal ranges start with a flat printed pattern so you will not be distracted by light and shadow as in a complete room.

In the photograph on this page there is a fabric with a well-defined strong pattern that contains several colors and tones. Around it are grouped together samples of plain fabrics in the same dark tones and the same pale tones that correspond to the colors in the fabric. The two main colors – pink and green – are in the same tonal range.

The differences in tonal range show up well in the black-and-white photograph. Note how the extremities of the range – the very light and the very dark tones – are used sparingly, and act as accents.

FEW COLORS/MANY TONES

Room schemes on a one-color (monochrome) theme need not be dull. You can make them visually effective by working with a range of shades from very pale to very intense, running through the entire tonal range.

Shadows When evaluating the tonal range don't forget to take into account areas of permanent shadow, such as the folds of drapery or the shadow cast by a large wardrobe. These obviously darken the tone of any color, adding an extra dimension to the tonal range.

▷ *One-color schemes*

While basically one color, this room works well because of its wide variety of tones. Here the intensely bright ribbon hanging down over the bed lifts the whole scheme and creates immediate and visual interest. White lacy cushions on the bed and a white paint job mark the opposite end of the tonal range.

◁ *Sea-misty*
A wide range of sea-green tones comes together to create a varied but restful mood.

▽ *The black-and-white photograph of the scene on the left clearly indicates the range of tones and how the areas of shadow created by the drapery add movement and variety to the overall scheme. The tone scale shows that every tone is included except black.*

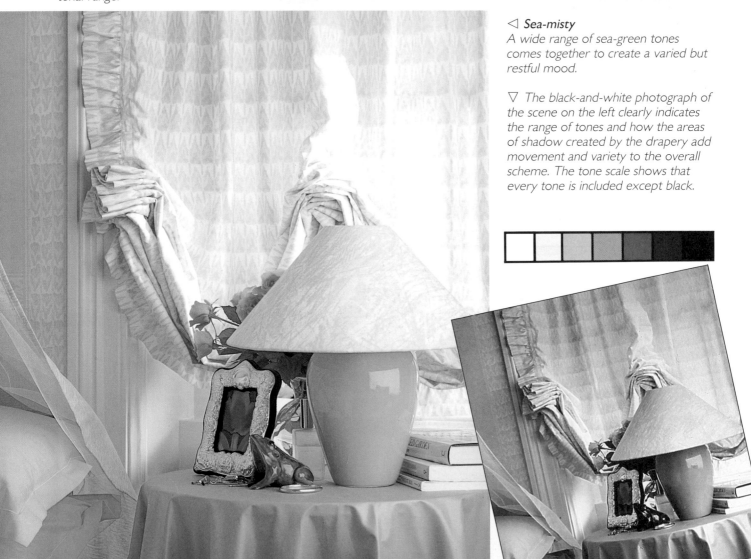

MANY COLORS/FEW TONES

A room scheme that combines too many colors can look busy and restless. However, if most of the colors are as close together as possible in the tone scale this will greatly help to calm and unify the whole scheme.

▷ Multi-colored schemes

This room is decorated in rich, mid-to-dark colors – predominantly terra-cotta, blues and greens. There are two differently patterned wallcoverings and a border, and several fabric patterns. Even the ceramic lamp and paper shade have the same rich colors, as do the various cushions that are dotted around the room for accent.

The reason that this works as a cohesive and harmonious scheme – rather than just looking like a mess – is because, apart from the white accents outlining the paisley patterns, the colors themselves come from a narrow tonal range – as can be seen below from the black-and-white print of the lamp corner on the desk.

▷ Warmth and light

Although of quite a different color, the mainly red lamp shade blends harmoniously into the background of mainly green fabric because – as can be seen from the black-and-white print – its tonal value is practically the same. In the evenings artificial light also plays a part in varying the tonal contrast, deepening shadows and highlighting the palest tones.

AVOIDING TONAL TRAPS

Sometimes it helps to see why schemes do *not* work, in order to understand how to avoid the obvious pitfalls. The left-hand column of drawings shows three common problems: the center column shows the problem in black and white terms; and the right-hand column shows one way to put the tonal balance right. Now try to imagine what colors should be used to produce the tones illustrated in the third column.

Bear in mind the tonal range of wood too. Whether it is light ash, mid oak, dark mahogany or stained black will affect the overall tonal balance of a scheme, just as much as the more obvious color differences.

Problem: spotty and stark
There are lots of intense red elements with black and white.

Tonal analysis *This scheme looks virtually all black and white, because intense colors are tonally very dark.*

Solution *Adding a mid-tone background – either on the walls or floors – helps to link extreme tones.*

Problem: too garish *This scheme includes several pastels and several intense colors.*

Tonal analysis *As well as a variety of colors, there is a wide range of tones from very light to very dark.*

Solution *To maintain a colorful scheme, it's best to stick to a narrow band of tones for the colors.*

Problem: bland and boring
All the colors are slavishly picked out from the blind fabric pattern.

Tonal analysis *Everything – walls, woodwork, floor and fabrics – are in the same light tone.*

Solution *Make sure walls or floors are slightly lighter or darker, and introduce a little tonal contrast as an accent.*

COLOR AND PROPORTION

Learn how to use colors – warm or cool, light or dark – to change the shape and feel of a room.

The way you use color on the six main areas of a room – the four walls, the floor and the ceiling – can dramatically or subtly alter the apparent proportions of the room. You can change how long a room looks, or how narrow or low it is, simply by the way you use color and tone.

First, you need to give the room in question a long hard look. Does it basically have good proportions, or does it leave something to be desired? Is the ceiling a bit too high or too low? Does the hall feel like a long dark tunnel? Is the floor space rather small? Does the room feel too large for the amount of furniture in it? Are there awkward or untidy features – such as a sloping ceiling or a recess – that break up the space in the room and make it feel cramped?

A dark floor covering defines the edges of a large room, making the floor appear smaller than it really is.

If the room is well proportioned, you will want to make sure that you use color and tone to enhance its good qualities. If the room needs help, the whole range of colors, from light to dark tones, are the home decorator's best friend.

CHARACTERISTICS OF COLOR

A color can make a surface appear closer or further away, and thus look smaller or larger in comparison to another color. Being aware of the visual effects of different colors and tones helps you to create the effect you want.

Cool colors, such as blue-green, blue or blue-lilac, tend to recede, pushing back the walls of a room and making it feel more spacious. Light colors recede too, so using a pale cool color creates the maximum illusion of space. Add a pale wall-to-wall carpet and you increase the sense of space even more, particularly if the baseboards are painted in a color similar to the carpet.

In contrast, walls painted in warm or dark colors seem closer. Large rooms with high ceilings can often feel spacious and unwelcoming, so painting the walls and ceiling in warm restful tones helps create a cozier and more relaxing atmosphere.

◁ *Raising the roof*
This scheme is limited to beiges, browns and grays, in subtle tones that range from dark to light. It shows clearly how tone can affect the shape and feel of a room. A light ceiling and floor increases the height of the room, and a soft mid-tone draws in the walls slightly. A dark border gives added definition.

ALTERING SPACE WITH COLOR

In high-ceilinged rooms, corridors or narrow rooms, you can change the proportions of space by contrasting dark floor and ceiling colors with light walls. This has the effect of appearing to lower the ceiling and increase the width of the room. In the same way, a long room appears shorter if the end wall is a warm rich color.

A room with a low ceiling may feel oppressive, but if the ceiling is a much lighter color than the walls, the room appears to be taller. Make sure that the walls are the same color right up to the ceiling, not just to the picture or plate rail level, for maximum effect.

Sometimes rooms are squeezed into awkward spaces, particularly in apartments converted from houses designed for more spacious living. Sloping ceilings, for example, can make a room feel cramped, but by blending the awkward shape in with the walls, you open up the space. Similarly, a recess can be drawn into a room by painting it in a warm or dark color.

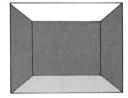

△ *Raising a ceiling*
To make a ceiling feel higher, paint it in a lighter color than the walls. In this rather box-shaped dining room the ceiling has been painted in brilliant white, in stark contrast with dark green walls. The light ceiling makes the room feel taller than it really is, and the dark tone draws the walls inward, creating an intimate atmosphere.

It is important that the color of the walls is continuous, right up to the height of the ceiling. If, for example, details such as the plate rail were picked out in another color, breaking up the wall, the effect would not be so successful.

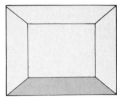

▷ *Making space*
This is the same dining room as the one above, with the same furniture and carpet, but it looks completely different.

The walls and the ceiling are painted in soft pastel colors – a very light apricot and rose white. There is far less contrast between ceiling and walls than in the dark green dining room. Instead of appearing taller, the pale colors push the walls back and make the room feel larger and more light and airy. The molding and plate rail are picked out in a slightly darker shade, to add definition.

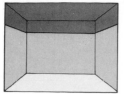

▷ *Lowering a ceiling*
Some rooms have ceilings that feel uncomfortably high for the size of the room. Painting the ceiling in a tone that is slightly darker than the walls makes it appear to be lower. The effect is increased if the ceiling color is painted down to the level of a picture or plate rail.

In this living room the problem is solved by painting the ceiling a dark ochre. Using the ceiling color to outline the wall panels anchors the paler walls against the dark ceiling, at the same time balancing a color scheme that could have been oppressive.

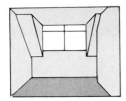

△ Disguising awkward shapes

Attic rooms such as this one feel cramped because a sloping ceiling creates awkward spaces. When decorating it's hard to know where the walls end and the ceiling begins: the ceiling will seem very low if the wallcovering ends where the slope begins. The best approach is to paint or cover the walls and ceiling in the same color to camouflage the awkward shape. In this room mini-print wallpaper covers all wall surfaces.

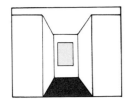

▷ Widening a narrow room

Corridors, galley kitchens and small single bedrooms tend to be narrow, but if painted in very pale colors they appear more spacious.

The all-white fitted cupboards and appliances create an illusion of space in this narrow kitchen. The white venetian blind over the window blends the window into the wall when closed adding to this illusion. White tiles with bright red spots add interest to the white decoration.

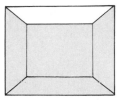

◁ **Making a room feel larger**
Pale colors reflect more light than dark colors, and cool colors recede. So a combination of the two is perfect for making a small room seem larger.

In this sunny little room, the walls, ceilings and floor are decorated in a range of cool pastels, creating a bright spacious airiness. Note that there are no great contrasts between colors to break up the overall effect. The woodwork of the window and the baseboards are painted in pale aqua colors and the wooden floor is sanded and stained.

In a room that doesn't get any sun, temperate colors – such as pale lemon-yellow or pale lilac-gray – would be a better choice. A wall-to-wall carpet in a soft neutral color is another way to add to the illusion of space, particularly if the baseboards are painted in a similar color. A neat window treatment, such as this roman blind, helps to keep the room uncluttered and spacious.

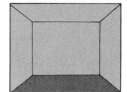

▷ **Making a large room cozier**
Spacious rooms can sometimes feel austere and unwelcoming, particularly if they get little sun. Choose a tone from the warm side of the color wheel – for both the ceiling and walls – to create a cheerful color scheme that draws the walls inward slightly and the ceiling downward, making the room feel more inviting. The strength of the tone is as important as the color itself, so use soft mid-tones for the best results. This large well-proportioned bedroom is painted in a soft rose pink to create a comfortable and restful atmosphere. The pink is warm enough to make the room feel cozier but not so strong that it becomes oppressive.

THE IMPORTANCE OF TONE

It's hard to notice the tonal relationships of colors when looking at color photographs of rooms. But it's the way in which light, medium or dark tones are used that affects the shape of a room, even more than the actual colors themselves.

These diagrams show at a glance how to achieve a range of different effects, highlighting points you like and disguising problems. If you make a tracing of this page you can color in the drawings to see how a variety of different colors – and different tones – look.

To make a room feel larger decorate in light colors. The lighter the color the more light is reflected and the larger the room feels.

To make a room feel smaller or cozier, use warm colors to bring the walls inward and the ceiling downward.

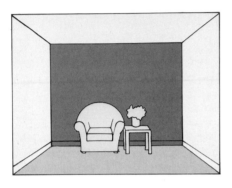

Dark colors and warm colors advance. A single wall painted in a dark color will be drawn into the room.

Cool colors recede. A wall painted in a light cool color appears farther away than it really is.

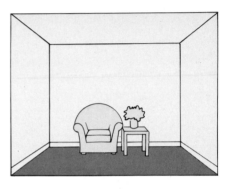

A dark floorcovering makes the floor seem smaller. It also defines the edges of the room and draws the eye downward.

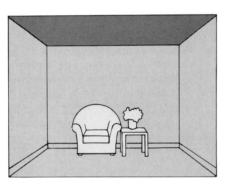

To lower a ceiling use a color that is slightly darker than the walls but not so dark that it feels oppressive.

To raise a ceiling use a color that is lighter than the walls. Increase the effect by painting the walls right up to the level of the ceiling.

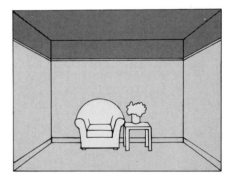

To lower a ceiling in a very large room paint the top section of the walls in the same dark color as the ceiling.

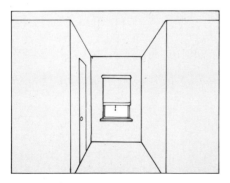

To widen a corridor use a very light color on the walls, ceiling and floor. The reflected light will make the space seem less confined.

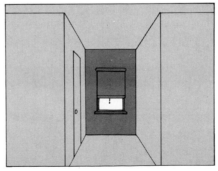

To shorten a corridor, or a long narrow room, paint the end wall in a dark or warm color, to make it appear closer.

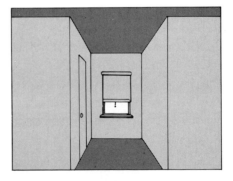

To change the proportions of a corridor, decorate the ceiling and floor in a darker color than the walls. The space will appear wider and lower.

THE EFFECT OF LIGHT ON COLOR

When planning a color scheme, it's important to know how natural and artificial light affect furnishings.

Professional interior designers and color consultants consider the direction a room faces. Whether it is north, south, east or west, makes a great deal of difference to the choice of color scheme. For instance, a bedroom that faces east and receives strong sunlight in the early morning will look very different when next seen late at night in artificial lighting. A west-facing room that has a warm glow in the evening can look dull in the mornings. Your choice of color should take this into account.

Of course, an ideal exposure is not always possible for everyone. City apartments may enjoy little naturally available light and be surrounded on all sides. A north-facing room can expect less sun than a south- or west-facing one, but whatever the exposure, with clever lighting and color scheming the interior can be made to feel welcoming and attractive.

The style of the house you live in can also make a great deal of difference to the amount of available light in an interior. A cottage-style house may be in a superbly sunny location but have low ceilings and tiny windows that can make the interior feel dark and gloomy. Modern homes with spacious open-plan interiors and large picture windows will be even more affected by their exposure, and seasonal changes. If there is a living room with a screened-in porch attached that is used as an additional seating area during the summer but not in winter, the decor will have to be flexible enough to accommodate the changes.

For people in doubt over lighting and color schemes some top interior designers suggest painting a room white before making a final color choice. This is a good way to observe how changes in natural light affect an interior and helps you make the most of it when choosing a color scheme. Some interior designers incorporate every kind of domestic light fixture into their showrooms so that clients can see the effect of different kinds of artificial light on carpets, fabrics and wallcoverings.

Diffused, even light

In order to take advantage of all the available light, skylights were installed across the expanse of ceiling and full-sized windows were placed on the north-facing wall. The room has a neutral color scheme with pastel touches. The rug ties it all together.

MATCHING FURNISHINGS

The most usual way to color match is to look at samples in the daylight. However, this doesn't enable you to judge the effect at home under artificial lighting conditions. Viewing samples under shop lights is also unsatisfactory as they mostly use color-corrected fluorescent tubes resembling daylight. Neither type of light will give an idea of the average home's incandescent lighting with its distinctive yellow cast. Carpets and textured fabrics are particularly vulnerable to change from artificial lighting. Synthetic fabrics that match perfectly in daylight may no longer do so under artificial light.

Fabric The effect of artifical lighting on curtains is better seen if a sample yard of fabric is pleated and held upright; looking at lamp shade fabrics lit from behind also gives a better idea.

Paint Window walls will appear darker since they only receive reflected light; ceilings always look darker than walls painted the same color. If in doubt use a shade lighter than your first choice; once all the walls are painted they tend to appear darker than the paint sample on a card.

Carpets Put samples flat on the floor and move them around the room to see how different positions and lighting conditions can affect the color.

△ ▷ *Lighting – day and night*
It's hard to believe that these two pictures are of the same living room. (Above) Natural daylight shows off the subtle, neutral color scheme of white and bluish grays in this modern interior. (Right) The same living room seen at night under artificial lighting. The yellow cast of incandescent lighting has turned the gray upholstery and carpet a yellow-beige and given the entire room a unifying, warm glow.

△ *Daylight*
Choosing colors by daylight can work well for rooms mainly in daytime use. But successful daytime color combinations may not work well at night.

△ *Fluorescent*
Some color-corrected fluorescents can give much the same effect as daylight. Other types of fluorescent have a cold, blue and harsh draining effect.

△ *Incandescent*
The lighting most commonly used in the home; it emphasizes the yellow-reds, so a coral and apricot color scheme will look much more intense.

△ *Incandescent halogen*
This has a much whiter light than pure incandescent and would benefit a neutral blue-gray color scheme more since there is less color distortion.

◁ **Peaches and corals for warmth**
North-facing rooms need to feel cozy. Although some primrose yellows may take on a greeny tinge and bright reds feel claustrophobic, soft, muted coral shades can work well in sponged, dragged or stippled paint techniques. Apricot or peach curtains at a window give a warm cast to white walls. A Chinese carpet with a coral background warms up the floor.

▽ **South-facing, cool neutrals**
A neutral color scheme using cool blue-grays works well in this situation. White sheer curtains at the window diffuse and filter strong sunlight and protect upholstery and carpet from the sun's rays.

△ **Cool blue mood**
This room feels typically Mediterranean with its tiled floor and cool, blue color scheme. Blue-lined curtains lend a cool cast to the walls. In winter these curtains could be changed to a warm peachy print with peach linings; loose covers in warm peach and beige could transform this into a warm, cozy color scheme.

▷ **North-facing using neutrals**
A semi-transparent blind cleverly provides privacy without blocking out too much daylight.
    The light tan soft leather seating looks warm while the neutral beige carpet and touches of coral in an abstract rug and picture also help to warm up this scheme.

Adding light A white gloss-painted ceiling is a wonderful light reflector and in a dark room can act like a mirror and significantly increase the amount of available light. However, gloss-painted ceilings *must* be perfect – free from paint drips and unsightly cracks and bumps since a high sheen also emphasizes less-than-perfect surfaces.

△ *North-facing but warm*
Although green is generally considered a cool color, the pale yellow-green on these walls combines successfully with a warm cream ceiling and the muted pink of the upholstery.

▽ *South-facing – using neutrals*
Browns appear less somber in a south-facing room because the yellow emphasis of sunlight brings out the red that is the basis for browns. White walls also take on a creamy look.

WORKING WITH PATTERNS

Using patterns needs as much careful consideration as using color to achieve successful results.

The number of patterns available in wallcoverings, fabrics and floorcoverings nowadays is enormous, ranging from simple geometrics and color spatter designs to formal florals. How to choose patterns and how to use them can be an awe-inspiring prospect, but once you have learned about the characteristics of different patterns, creating the atmosphere or style you want becomes easier.

Pattern is an essential ingredient in any room scheme. It plays a part in creating the style and in enhancing the color scheme, whether it is used in small areas – cushions, decorative paper borders or tiles, for example – or over much larger areas such as wallcoverings, ceilings and floors.

The strength of pattern should not be underestimated. Designs in a single bold color appear to be more striking and imposing than a plain surface painted in the same color. In the same way, a rather delicate pale color is given more life on a patterned surface.

Scale is an important consideration, too. Large-scale designs can be wasted on the walls of small rooms, for instance, particularly if the wallcovering has a motif that is cut off in awkward places; and small bright designs tend to look busy.

On the next two pages patterned materials are divided up into eight different categories to provide a guide to the vast range of designs available.

Single color
Mixing all sorts of patterns together can be risky, but relating them to each other by choosing designs in the same color is one way of making a successful combination.

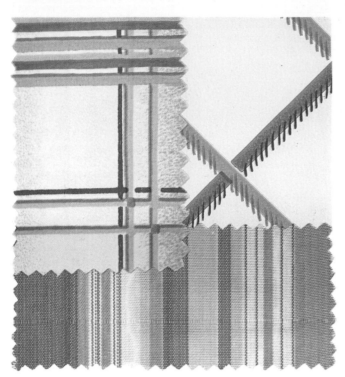

Checks, stripes and trellis

These patterns are some of the oldest and most striking designs. There are hundreds of variations in all colors, which can be traditional or modern in style – checks can be simple black and white squares, gingham or tartan, for example. A touch of one of these simple patterns makes a good accent in solid color schemes.

Spots and spatters

These designs have a very modern feel to them. Spots can be regularly spaced or randomly printed, large or small. Spatter-patterns imitate the effects of tiny droplets of paint splashed and dribbled across the wall. Strong colors can be mixed together to create lively and vibrant combinations.

Floral

Patterns range from large-scale oriental designs and traditional chintzes to splashy watercolor designs and very simple modern prints. The more dense florals need to be used in large rooms, but the softer colors and looser designs suit most rooms. They look good combined with solids that draw out the tones of the designs.

Abstract

A collection of modern patterns used in wallcoverings and fabrics. They have no recognizable motifs, such as flowers, plants or birds; instead they are made up of random shapes – splotches, freehand zigzags, torn paper shapes or combinations of crooked lines and gentle swirls of color, for instance, in all sorts of color combinations.

Geometric
The designs are made up of shapes such as triangles, chevrons, diamonds and key patterns. They come in all sizes and combinations of colors to create different effects – a crisp tailored look can be made by using geometrics for wallcoverings and window dressings, for instance. These designs often work well with mini prints and florals.

Exotic
The designs are based on traditional patterns from all over the world – India, Asia, Africa, the Pacific and the Americas. Rich colors and textures are combined in bold patterns – stripes, geometric or floral designs, or simple images of people and animals. Chinese designs are in delicate colors; Indian and African patterns are dark and rich.

Mini print
Wallcoverings and fabrics are available in a wide variety of colors and patterns, including flower sprigs, florals and geometrical shapes. They can have a traditional country feel to them and are especially suitable for small rooms where it would be easy for a larger patterned wallcovering to be overwhelming.

Textural
These designs are printed to imitate other materials, such as wood grain, and various paint effects including stippling, sponging, dragging, rag rolling or marbling, and fabrics, such as moiré silk. These patterns give large flat surfaces, particularly walls, more visual interest and a luxurious feel without being overpowering.

△ *Daisy design*
A wallpaper and fabric design of Michaelmas daisies – a pattern created at the end of the 19th century by the famous English designer William Morris – makes a cozy atmosphere in this living room without feeling overwhelming. A plain carpet provides a neutral background for the wealth of pattern and the deep pink cushions act as accents.

◁ *Floral tradition*
The small, rather old-fashioned floral design on the wallpaper and fabric looks light and airy in this pretty bedroom. The eyelet lace bed trim adds to the traditional feel of the room.

ALL-OVER PATTERN

It is difficult to imagine what a pattern will look like over a large area when you are working from a sample. The main points to consider are the colors in the pattern, the type of design and its size.

Small designs, such as flower sprigs in pastel tones, can disappear on the walls of a large room – some even look like solids or textures from a distance. On the other hand, a small but boldly colored geometric makes a strong impact – this may be just the effect you want in a large and unwelcoming room, but it could be oppressive in a small room.

The type of design also affects the style of a room. If you are looking for a period atmosphere, go for traditional florals, Regency stripes, or paint effects, such as marbling, not brightly colored geometrics, spots or checks.

◁ *Blue all over*
This simple color scheme mixes mid-blue with the warm natural tones of wood and cane. The room is large and light enough to take the large-scale paisley pattern on the walls and ceiling without feeling dark or cramped.

71

△ Pastel patterns

The bed is the biggest piece of furniture in a bedroom, so the bedspread is an important part of the decorating scheme, especially when using a single pattern throughout the room. The effect could easily be overpowering if not carefully planned.

This large-scale check in soft pastels – blue, mauve, pink, orange and yellow – is used in matching fabrics and wallcovering. It is an unusual but refreshing color scheme for a bedroom.

▷ Spots and stripes

The mini-print design (right) – in soft gray with spots of pastel tones, or the boldly colored exotic stripe (left) – called ikat and based on the patterns created by American Indians – provide two very different bedroom color schemes.

USING PATTERNS WITH SOLIDS

With just one pattern as the focal point in a room, there is a variety of ways to use solid colors.

If you feel unsure about mixing and matching wallcovering patterns, then using one design with accompanying solid colors is the best way of building up an attractive and individual room scheme. Varying shades of one color, or two or even three different colors picked from the chosen pattern can be used on walls and floor, upholstery and curtains. The many choices open to you for both paint color and solid colored fabrics leave plenty of leeway to create different moods according to personal preference.

Textures, too, can be varied: a shiny chintz that reflects the light, or a rough, nubby tweed that absorbs it, can create quite different effects even when they are the same color.

If the pattern is in the upholstery, plain curtains edged with one other color from the design look smart and sophisticated. Alternatively, if it is the curtains that are patterned, pick one of the colors in a self-patterned material for upholstery, with contrast piping and cushions in the curtain fabric.

Painted walls can be given added in-terest; the technique known as dragging adds depth to the color, while the techniques of ragging and sponging allow the introduction of two complementary color shades that can be picked to tone with the fabric pattern.

Another possibility, of course, is that you have chosen a strongly patterned wallcovering and wish to keep it as the main feature in your room. In this case, pick out two of the main colors for solid, tailored curtains or blinds.

Red as background

This sitting/bedroom demonstrates a balance of solid and patterned decor. The brightly painted solid red walls and white window trim contrast a flowery black rug and similar window treatments. The leafy vine border found below the molding introduces yet another pattern and color.

To help you decide which colors to pick for individual treatment, it's a good idea to match up some paint samples to the different colors in the pattern. Cut them out and look at them against a neutral background.

A multi-colored fabric gives you a huge variety of colors to choose from: first, the shades that match precisely those contained in the pattern; second, a range of pastel tones in the same colors to soften the overall room scheme; and third, darker shades.

Those colors that are most pleasing to you – either because of their vibrancy or their soothing nature – are the ones to pick out for cushions, carpet or walls.

△ *Colorful choice*
A really colorful curtain fabric offers a wide range of color choices for other surfaces in the room. Here is a selection of some of the solid fabrics and paint colors that could successfully be used to accompany it.

▷ *Bright and cheerful*
Jazzy modern interpretation of a floral print draws the eye immediately to the window and the view beyond. Yellow walls keep up the cheerful feeling set by the bright curtains. Contrasting lavender-blue cushions pick up another of the colors within the pattern, while the gray carpet subtly reflects the mauvish tint.

△ **Summertime blues**
Focusing on the blues, a cooler scheme is created by putting very pale blue on the walls but a richer blue on the floor.

△ **Springtime freshness**
Picking out two different colors – palest pink walls and a mossy green carpet – brings a touch of spring to the room.

△ **Reversing the scheme**
The muted design on the wall is echoed in the cream curtains, gray carpet and reverse contrast-piped cushions.

▷ The wallpaper and fabric samples used in the room above. A self-patterned cream weave adds an interesting texture.

△ **Bright and light**
A deep blue background with a bright multi-colored floral design forms the basis for an unusual bedroom scheme. Echoing pastel tints on the sofa soften the overall effect. On the right are some of the shades that could be picked out of the pattern to use in a color scheme. Different textures for upholstery and curtains or cushions result in a different effect.

DECORATING WITH MINI PRINTS

Some of the most versatile patterns are the tiny, all-over designs that are not only pretty but also make good camouflage.

Mini prints were in vogue as soon as the first printed wallcoverings and fabrics appeared in the 18th century. Their almost doll's house scale suited the contemporary Georgian homes and their elegant furniture. The Victorians, too, favored tiny, all-over, sprigged designs and frequently used them to great effect. Toward the end of the 19th century, however, mini print popularity declined in favor of larger, bolder patterns.

It wasn't until the 1970s that overall mini prints really came back into fashion. Firms such as Laura Ashley started to introduce them in lines of closely color coordinated wallcoverings and furnishing fabrics that were largely inspired by both 18th century and Indian wood-block designs. They included sprigs of flowers, widely spaced motifs and trellis patterns.

These small, pretty prints allowed people who had never before dared to mix patterns in a room to try their hand at it with success. Tile manufacturers then followed suit by matching their lines to wallcoverings and fabrics so schemes could be completely coordinated. Carpet manufacturers completed the mini-pattern revolution by introducing tiny all-over designs.

HOW TO USE THEM

There is a practical aspect to decorating with mini prints. They are particularly successful at camouflaging unevenly plastered wall surfaces – small all-over patterns break up large areas by preventing the eye from concentrating on one spot and seeing the flaws. All-over mini-patterned carpets are also excellent for rooms that get heavy wear, particularly hallways, as they tend not to show the dirt as easily as solid-colored ones.

However, mini prints do need to be chosen with care. They can be overpowering if the color contrast between background and pattern is too marked. Small patterns may also lose definition in a large room but can be more successful when used in combination with a larger scale print.

Muted background

The mini-printed paper here is highly reminiscent of 18th century style both in design and colorings. The muted beige background makes a gentle contrast in relation to the motif, making the overall effect easy on the eye and a good backdrop for dark furniture.

△ **Traditional blue and white**
Mini prints blend well with traditional furnishings and suit older homes and small rooms particularly well. Mixing different designs together is easier if you stick to matching colors.

▷ **Mixing two together**
A white, leopard-spotted canopy adorns the bed. The curtains and night table boast mini spots and flowers partnered with a faux rug. Walls and accents are white and pink.

HOW TO CHOOSE

In a shop where all you have to choose from is a sample book, it can sometimes be difficult to imagine how large expanses of a small design will look on a wall or hanging at your window. Whenever possible, try to see a big piece of the wallcovering or fabric. Stand away from it squinting slightly to get the effect. Some shops have made choosing mini prints easier by covering large display panels that can be viewed at a distance.

On wide-spaced mini prints, that is, those with large areas of background color in between the motifs, the spaces themselves start becoming more important and even form their own patterns within the design.

Geometric designs need to be considered very carefully. If your walls are slightly askew, a mini print of this kind tends to emphasize it – especially if the pattern contains stripes as well. A

pretty, overall floral design, on the other hand, can help disguise bumpy walls.

Mini prints whose colors are closer in tonal value tend to merge together, whereas high color contrasts look busier and crisper. Spaced sprigs with contrasting tones look even more widely spaced than ever. Generally speaking, this type of design looks better in smaller room schemes where there's not much furniture or clutter.

As a more modern alternative to creating a romantic atmosphere with pastel flower sprigs, look for more geometric designs. Some of these geometrics can perhaps be held within stripes as they give a more formal look. In common with sponging and stippling, mini prints can soften dramatic expanses of wall and window color by giving a more muted, dappled impression. They can also be used to introduce strong color into a scheme.

TYPES OF MINI PRINT

Mini prints come in a variety of looks, styles and patterns. It's important to understand the different effects that can be created when the same pattern is viewed close up and from a distance of around two yards away.

△ *Dark and light*
A fabric or wallcovering with a predominantly red background brings walls and windows closer; white backgrounds make areas feel comparatively light.

△ *Close together sprigs*
Over large areas, widely spaced designs can sometimes give a restless, 'dotted' effect whereas 'close together' prints can make small rooms feel claustrophobic.

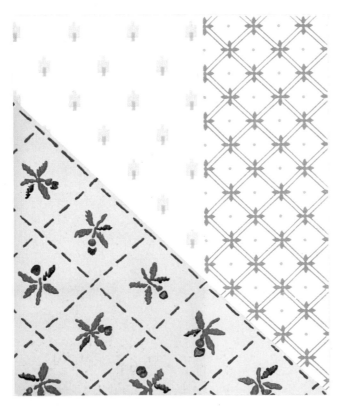

△ *Geometric*
These prints can offset fussy all-over mini floral patterns, giving the eye a break and making a mini print scheme feel more restful.

△ *Contrast and close tones*
Motifs in colors that are similar in tone to their backgrounds simplify complex, busy patterns and give a pleasantly muted effect to large expanses of wall or curtain.

Prints here are two-thirds actual size

△ *Stripes and florals*
A combination of stripes, florals and mini prints can be used successfully if the colors are coordinated correctly. In this room, a red floral mini print is the backdrop for a red floral sofa accented with striped throw pillows and a striped lamp shade. The key to this decor is the red, white and blue color scheme.

▷ *Cheerful open sprigs*
A brightly contrasting striped print in red and white combined with a wide-spaced sprig pattern could be overpowering. However, the pale green leaves in the pattern bring relief by offsetting the sharp contrast. Adding a splash of deeper green plants makes the whole scheme feel more restful.

◁ △ *Patterned and solid*
This bedroom's deep blue-green wallpaper is broken up by the overall design of twining white flowers (see detail). A colorful patchwork tablecloth echoes the floral mini print design, while solid blinds and curtains offset any busy feeling.

▽ *Patterns for camouflage*
All-over prints can help to disguise odd corners, awkward angles and uneven surfaces often found in older homes. Coordinating fabrics on the bed and at the window help to give a unified feel.

USING TEXTURES EFFECTIVELY

Learn how to use textures – rough or smooth, matte or shiny, hard or soft – to bring life to your color schemes.

Texture describes how any material feels to the touch. Every surface has a texture. If you compare, for example, the surfaces of a telephone and a kettle you will find that although both appear to be smooth they have quite different textures. The plastic has a warm feel to it, and is slightly brittle, but the metal of the kettle is cold and hard.

Texture can be visual as well as something you can feel. Painting techniques such as stippling, sponging, dragging or rag-rolling create interesting visual textures on a smooth surface.

Deciding on which texture to use is as important a part of decorating as choosing colors because texture has as much effect on the different elements in a room and the overall atmosphere. A haphazard collection of textures can be as unsuccessful as an unbalanced color scheme, so think carefully about the materials you plan to use and the surfaces – walls, floor, ceiling, furnishings – you are going to cover.

CHOOSING TEXTURES

Textures are loosely divided into two groups – rough and smooth – which provoke quite different reactions. Rough textures, such as brick, wood, sisal, wicker or suede, have a rustic homey feel about them. At the opposite extreme, the smoothness of glass, the hardness of chrome and the glossiness of plastic, for instance, bring a hard-edged look to a room.

You can create successful schemes using mixtures that are at neither one extreme nor the other. It's similar to mixing several different tones of one color rather than just using dark or light ones.

Texture is also used in the same way as accents of color. In a well balanced but perhaps slightly boring color scheme you can inject a little interest by adding a contrasting texture. Similarly, if a whole room is decorated using smooth textures, adding some rougher surfaces will create a lively contrast.

HOW TEXTURE AFFECTS COLOR

Texture is linked closely to color. The quality of a color – its richness or brightness, for instance – varies depending on the texture of the surface.

Smooth surfaces reflect light and dull ones absorb it. So the color painted in latex on a wall looks lighter than the same color used in a heavy woven fabric. Compare for yourself two objects in the same color which have different textures – a red towel and a red plastic soap dish, for example – and you will see how the color is affected.

Combing textures

In this living area, polished chrome contrasts dramatically with the heavy, tweed sofa cover. Suede chair covers, cotton draperies and a Berber carpet add less extreme textures.

WALLS

The walls of a room are the largest surface area to decorate and there are literally thousands of different ways of treating them. Wallcoverings, paints, fabrics and tiles all provide a wide selection of different textures.

Wallcoverings are available in all kinds of finishes that range from smooth and gleaming foils to rich flocks and embossed papers, such as anaglypta or woodchip, and vinyls that imitate textures such as moiré or raw silk; and real fabrics, such as burlap, wool, silk, linen or cork.

Paints come in several finishes, too – silk or matte latex for walls, and gloss or semi gloss for woodwork. There are plenty of painting techniques that add visual texture to the surface of a wall but are less overpowering than a tangible texture such as burlap or anaglypta. Rag-rolling creates an effect like soft, crushed silk, stippling looks like the texture of orange peel, and sponging, using two or three colors, can produce a wide range of mottled effects.

WINDOWS

The texture of window dressings, whether they are curtains with swags and jabots or mirror venetian blinds, play an important part in creating the atmosphere of a room. Fabrics with a deep pile, such as velvet, suggest warmth; the sharp outline of a venetian blind has a cool businesslike quality to it; a neatly folding roman blind in cotton comes somewhere between the two.

The choice ranges from rich velvets to light, billowing sheers – and can include materials like muslin or felt.

The texture of window dressings is more pronounced because light not only shines on them but through them, too. The texture can be enhanced by the way the fabric is hung. Pleating or ruching, for example, creates a play of light and shadow on the surface of the fabric.

You don't have to limit yourself to one fabric per window. Layers of different texture and pattern can be combined – a roller blind with curtains, two or three curtains of different weights, or draped fabric with blinds. The layers – say, lace, cotton and satin – are drawn back in stages to show off the different textures.

FLOORS

The floor is the surface we are in most contact with and so the texture of the floor surface – whether it feels rough or smooth, warm or cold, hard or soft – is as important as the choice of color and any practical considerations.

Carpets can be smooth, knobby, sculpted, or flecked to create visual texture; rugs, rush, sisal, wood or cork flooring all have a warm feel to them; quarry tiles, ceramic tiles, marble and slate are hard cool surfaces.

The floor is frequently the starting point for a decorating scheme. Using several different materials, wall-to-wall carpet, sisal, wood and quarry tiles, perhaps, would make the overall effect in a house more interesting than if the same material had been used throughout.

In houses where rooms have more than one function, a change in the texture of the flooring can indicate the different uses of the space. For example, a kitchen/dining room could be laid with quarry tiles, with a floor rug under the table and chairs to bring warmth to the area that does not need to be so functional.

OTHER SURFACES

Apart from the walls, floors and windows, there are many other surfaces to consider in a decorative scheme.

Furniture can combine all kinds of textures. Wood is a very versatile surface. Wood furniture can be shiny and highly polished, or smooth with a matte finish, bleached, or pickled to bring out the grain, stained with a satin finish, or waxed to produce a subtle luster or a hard glossy shine.

Wood laminates, which are smooth and hardwearing, are good for use in the kitchen. Other plastic laminates with a variety of surfaces – smooth, satin and matte stripes, marble effect, for example – are used for kitchen countertops too.

Sofas and chairs can be covered in any number of furnishing fabrics ranging from nubby tweeds, ribbed velvets, linen, glazed cottons, to leather and suede. Cane and rush seats are combined with wood or contrasted with chrome, and cane furniture provides an alternative to wood.

Hard smooth surfaces such as glass and chrome create strong contrasts when combined with softer fabrics, but add to the smooth high-tech feel of leather, studded rubber or stainless steel.

NATURAL TEXTURES

The nubby surface of a Berber carpet, the roughness of un-polished wood or cork, the softness of woolen fabrics are just a few of the natural textures that help to create a warm homey atmosphere in a room.

In the inviting interior shown above a limited range of colors — beige, terra-cotta, cream and white — and the lack of any strong pattern show off the variety of surface textures. The smooth finish of the nest of pale oak tables, the picture frames and the painted paneling complement the rough surface of the sisal floor, the wool weave cover on the sofa and the glazed cotton cushions.

Notice how there are no extreme contrasts between textures. The sisal floor has a herringbone pattern that adds interest to a plain scheme without dominating it by being too strong. In the same way, the wood, although highly polished, does not have the cold hardness of metals such as brass or stainless steel.

The combination of real textures, some rougher than others, and visual textures — such as the grain of the wooden picture frames and the oak tables — is successful because it is well balanced, creating a comfortable feel to the room. Lighting is important here too. A soft light enhances the differences between surface textures.

△ **Rough and ready**
Pale cream wool weave, dark peach glazed cotton, sisal and polished maple and oak make a comfortable mixture of real and visual textures.

SMOOTH SURFACES

Chrome, glass, marble, mirror, brass, ceramic and stainless steel are just some of the materials that have very hard, smooth surfaces. But not all very smooth surfaces are hard; materials, such as vinyl, plastic laminates and leather, can have some flexibility in them, too.

Smooth textures can be shiny or matte; most shiny finishes, such as chrome, brass and mirror have a cold feel; in contrast, most matte surfaces, such as vinyl, stained wood or painted latex walls have some warmth in them.

A room that is made up entirely of smooth materials tends to have a hard-edged, even austere look to it. The dining room shown here is decorated with a variety of materials with smooth surfaces – chrome, perforated metal, vinyl, glass and stained wood – using a limited range of colors. The strong contrast between the colors – the black of the stained wood table and the white walls, for example – emphasizes the surface textures. The simple lines of the furniture bring this out, too. Look at the straight lines, sharp angles and geometric shapes, such as the glass and chrome side tables like cubes. The checked pattern of the vinyl floor makes an ideal background for this hard-edged linear scheme – although the effect is slightly softened by the use of gray rather than black with white.

△ **Going to extremes**
Polished chrome, glass, glazed china and vinyl combine matte and shiny finishes on smooth surfaces to give a hard-edged look.

△ **Rough and smooth**
Polished wood, a rag rug, crisp lace and china with a pretty floral design combine with hardwearing, smooth melamine (a laminate) and a shiny glazed tile.

FUNCTIONAL BUT COMFORTABLE

A combination of rough and smooth textures makes a well-balanced room scheme. Practicality often plays a part. A deep pile carpet might seem perfect for a bathroom – warm and luxurious – but it's not very practical when there's a lot of water about. A ceramic tile or vinyl floor is a good alternative because these materials are waterproof.

A kitchen needs to be practical but it doesn't have to be high-tech. This kitchen achieves a balance between warm, homey textures – such as wood and cotton – and functional, hardwearing surfaces. The cupboards and work surfaces are finished in smooth white melamine (a laminate) with pale turquoise glazed wall tiles. The floor, which looks fresh and easy to clean, is painted in a matching blue with a white border and topped with a striped rug, which adds some warmth to the smooth floor without being impractical.

A simple cotton curtain hangs from a wood pole above the striped wood window frame. Notice that a roller blind in a contrasting fabric has been used as well. A rustic touch is added with the smooth striped pine kitchen chairs and table covered with a finely woven white cloth with a pretty but simple lacy border.

MIX-AND-MATCH PATTERNS

Mixing several patterns together successfully in one room is now much simpler than it used to be.

Until recently, mixing patterns together in a room scheme required an excellent eye for color and self-confidence to carry through ideas. Coordinating a striped wallpaper with floral fabric and all the attendant accessories meant traipsing around shops with sample swatches, hoping that your purchase would match the original.

These days, more and more manufacturers are producing comprehensive mix-and-match lines of fabric, wallcoverings, borders – even trimmings.

These lines allow for the creation of much more exciting room schemes without the risk of a disaster because they are intended to harmonize, even though the designs vary. They can include floral patterns, spots, stripes and solid colors – very often with a 'moiré' look or self-patterned weave in an upholstery-weight fabric.

△ **Sample board**
Fabric and wallpaper samples used to build up the room scheme on the left.

◁ **Background link**
This warm beige background along with a main pattern of apricot and blue flowers has a 'moiré-look' design. This is repeated on the wallpaper, which also echoes the apricot flowers. The table is covered with two cloths, both with a self-pattern. The top one is spotted and the bottom one has a moiré design to coordinate with the overall theme.

△ Geometrics

Four different zigzag designs of muted neutrals combine to make a strikingly modern bedroom scheme. The vertical sawtooth pattern on the walls is echoed in the zigzags of the bedding and adjoining wall, and the more intricate herringbone on the reverse of the duvet cover introduces a lighter element into the overall picture while maintaining the geometric theme.

◁ Trellis and flowers

A bright geometric trellis design forms a natural background to a floral pattern that employs the same colors. Although two quite different styles of design, this combination works successfully because of the association of flowers with trelliswork and because the two principal colors are an exact match, coming from the same manufacturer. The small repeat of the trellis in the wallpaper border breaks up the large expanse of wall.

PLANNING A SCHEME

When choosing a coordinated room scheme where all the design elements come from one range, first decide which pattern is likely to be needed in the largest amount. In most cases this is the wallcovering and the curtain fabric.

When considering the walls, there are further decisions to be made before your final choice. For example, will you need two wallcoverings – above and below a chair rail, perhaps? Would you like to use a border – either to emphasize an architectural feature or to break up a featureless expanse?

With this settled you can then turn to the trimmings, details and finishing touches. If the curtains are long, would tiebacks enhance their appearance? If so, pick the same fabric or choose a matching one in a smaller design, and plan to repeat this in cushions or perhaps a tablecloth. If you want to dress the windows even more elaborately, consider adding a blind to match the tiebacks; there also may be a place for a window seat. Plain upholstery can be piped with contrasting colors.

△ **Building up**
Lightly patterned wallpaper of scattered leaves is topped by a more elaborate border – used again, but in reverse, above the picture rail. Colors in the curtain fabric are stronger, making them the dominating feature in the room.

Picking out the picture rail and cove molding in a paint that matches the color of the wallpaper motif not only turns it into an interesting feature in its own right but is also a useful device for visually lowering the room height.

◁ **Eye-catching abstract**
Two vivid abstract designs can still harmonize if they contain the same colors and tones. Here, the pale straw background is repeated in the carpet, forming a soft, neutral contrast to the busy fabrics.

△ Mini prints
The common denominator here is the wallpaper design consisting of small sprigged flowers, which is repeated and then printed over with larger, stronger-colored flowers in the fabric used for both blind and window seat. This emphasizes the window so that it is separated from, yet blended with, the walls.

▷ Checks and flowers
In all, there are five different patterns, from geometrical checks and stripes to a large floral design and a leafy mini print, combined to make this harmonious bedroom scheme. This scheme works because all the fabrics come from the same dye lot. The pastel tones impart a quiet air to what could have been a busy mixture of design and color.

△ **Sample board**
Samples of the five linked designs in the room shown at left.

△ **Sophisticated country**
Rich raspberry self-patterned chintz forms a perfect backdrop to old wood, while the flowery cushions echo the furniture's country feel. The designs are held together by rich pink, which appears throughout, and the three-berry motif on both wallpapers and floral cushion covers

▷ **Simply elegant**
An elegant little breakfast corner has been created by keeping to two colors – blue and white – and two motifs – flower sprigs and tiny spots. The simple chairs and cupboard are painted and the cupboard doors are covered with wallpaper

93

HOW TO BUILD UP A MIX-AND-MATCH SCHEME

Taking a window feature as an example, the illustrations show how an overall coordinated room scheme can be built up. Start with walls and draperies, then add festoons and a window seat, and finally the finishing touches of wallpaper border and cushions. Samples of the fabrics and wallcoverings used in the scheme are shown below.

△ **Stage 1** – Coordinating wallpaper and curtains are chosen, hung and draped with matching tiebacks.

△ **Stage 2** – A third coordinating design is added for festoon blinds and trimly piped cushions in the alcove.

△ **Stage 3** – Pillows introduce a fourth design, echoed in the border that neatly skirts the edge of the wallpaper.

INDEX

PHOTOGRAPHIC CREDITS
Simon Butcher/Eaglemoss, 31
Camera Press, 87
Camera Press/IMS, 14
Collier Campbell, 91 (bottom)
Coloroll, 1, 21, 90 (top)
Cover Plus from Woolworth, 41 (top), 57 (top)
Crown Paints, 46 (bottom), 48
Crown Wallcoverings, 81 (bottom)
Designers Guild, 16
Hazel Digby/Eaglemoss, 51
Dorma, 76
Dulux, 2, 3, 37, 44 (top), 56, 57 (bottom), 65
Phillip H. Ennis Photography, front cover, 38 (bottom), 43, 73, 79, 81 (top)
EWA/Michael Dunne, 39 (top), 71 (bottom), 71 (bottom), 83
EWA/Clive Helm, 62, 63, 66 (bottom)
EWA/Di Lewis, 92 (top)
EWA/Michael Nicholson, 64 (top)
EWA/Spike Powell, 58 (bottom), 66 (top right), 82 (top)
Habitat, 39 (bottom), 49, 64 (bottom), 72
Interior Selection, 90 (bottom)
Ken Kirkwood, 66 (top)
Michael Boys, 59 (bottom)
Melabee Miller, 19, 24, 61
National Magazine Co/Jan Baldwin, 77
National Magazine Co/David Brittain, 12 (top), 32, 41 (bottom), 86
Next Interior, 23, 34, 52-3
Osborne and Little, 55
Paper Moon Ltd., 67
PWA International, 33, 58 (top)
Quaker Maid, 40 (bottom)
Arthur Sanderson and Sons Ltd, 6, 15, 35, 45. 71 (top), 89
Sara Taylor/Eaglemoss, 4, 5, 9, 84, 85
Schreiber, 88
John Suett/Eaglemoss, 17, 18, 42
Swish Products Ltd, 74
Syndication International/Homes and Gardens, 44 (bottom)
Syndication International/Ideal Home, 10, 46 (top)
Syndication International/Woman and Home, 78
Texas Homecare, 12 (bottom)
The Picture Library, 93 (bottom)
Jerry Tubby/Eaglemoss, 7, 59 (top), 92 (bottom)
Village, 38 (top)
Vymura International, 82 (bottom)
Bryan Yates, 93 (top)

DESIGNER CREDITS
American Home Sewing & Crafts Association, 81
Pauline Boardman, Pauline Boardman, LTD., 38
Samuel Botero Associates, cover
Rosemarie Cicio, Rosemarie Cicio Interiors, 61
George Constant, George Constant Interior Design, 73
Elizabeth Gillin, ASID, Elizabeth Gillin Interiors, 24
J. Allen Murphy & Associates, 43, 79
Susan Rosenthal, ISID, 19